The Real Story Behind ERP:
Separating Fiction from Reality

Shaun Snapp

The Real Story Behind ERP: Separating Fiction from Reality

For information about this title or to order other books and/or electronic media, contact the publisher:
SCM Focus Press
PO Box 29502 #9059
Las Vegas, NV 89126-9502
http://www.scmfocus.com/scmfocuspress
(408) 657-0249

ISBN: 978-1-939731-24-1

Printed in the United States of America

Cover and interior design by: 1106 Design

Contents

CHAPTER 1

Introduction to ERP Software

This book was hatched during a conversation with a longtime friend who works in SAP Basis—the infrastructure area of SAP that is concerned with installing and maintaining the SAP applications. During our conversation he made the following comment:

> *"Look at the typical SAP landscape at a company. It now has so many applications that it eliminates what was supposed to be the advantage of ERP in the first place."*

My friend's statement got me thinking: what is actually known about the benefits of ERP? ERP significantly predates my introduction to working on IT projects, and because ERP has been on every project in which I have been involved, I have never actually seen a project **without** an ERP system. Quite simply, ERP has been ubiquitous and an unquestioned necessity. Certainly, I don't recall people saying they **liked** any of the ERP systems that had been on these projects, but that did not really matter; ERP was just the reality.

After this conversation with my colleague, I began researching the topic of ERP's usefulness and value-add to companies. I expected to find a large number of books—and quantities of research and articles—that demonstrated the benefits of ERP. Instead I found quite the opposite. Here is a synopsis of what I found:

1. There are few research studies on the benefits of ERP. The research that does exist shows that ERP has a low financial payback.

2. Research into multiple aspects of ERP by serious researchers (not some survey by a consulting company or IT analyst firm) clearly shows that ERP significantly changes companies, but that the benefits from these changes are of a dubious nature. That is, there can be a mixture of positive and negative outcomes from ERP implementations.

3. The actual research is at complete odds with most articles on ERP, which **almost universally promote ERP as a virtue.**

4. Most of the information on ERP is unsubstantiated hyperbole written by people who benefit financially from ERP implementations directly, or by those who have "sampled the Kool-Aid" and simply don't question any of the assumptions about ERP.

5. There are no books that question the benefits of ERP.

6. There is no book on the history of ERP.

What I discovered through my research was that my colleague's single observation was only the tip of the iceberg, only one example of what turned out to be multiple false assumptions about ERP put forward by multiple entities over many years. I actually held several false assumptions regarding the benefits of ERP myself; I had never analyzed the issue closely, and had been fed a steady stream of misinformation about ERP by biased parties and those who simply repeated the message they had heard from others. However, after I read the academic research on ERP, I was appalled to find unsubstantiated statements about ERP made repeatedly and routinely by individuals who presented themselves in their articles as knowing something about the ERP market. Of all the technologies I have researched, the coverage about ERP that I found was probably the worst journalism I have ever encountered. In fact, based on my research, I concluded that the vast majority of articles on ERP are misleading and not useful to people who are attempting to truly understand ERP. Of course, the articles are extremely useful to companies that wish to **sell ERP** software or services. Interestingly, ERP is a topic that has not been analyzed critically outside of the academic literature.

For those who believe that—at any time, at any place—the best determining factor of what is true is what most people think, this will not be a good book for you. Examples of when the prevailing opinion is incorrect are simply too easy to point out for anyone to be able to propose that generally agreed-upon opinions are correct. For instance, at one time, various gods explained all physical phenomena. In ancient Egypt there was a wind god, a sun god, a god of the harvest, a god that ate the sun in the evening and gave birth to the moon, and did the opposite in the morning. In ancient times people literally believed that physical phenomena could be controlled by praying to or making offerings to these gods. If that example is from a time too long ago for you, consider this: within the past one hundred years, the most prestigious universities in the US declared that women could never work in medicine because they would become hysterical at the sight of blood. More recently, US intervention in other countries was based upon a "domino theory," a proposal that was never proven, never meant to be proven, and was simply a justification for the violation of most of the treaties that the US had signed. These are the tip of the iceberg with respect to beliefs that were widely held and later proven to be false. So it is only too easy to find unsubstantiated beliefs that were broadly accepted in the past.

Examples of trends or transformations exist that were at one time entirely logical; the application of the steam turbine comes to mind. However, there are also many examples of supremely bad ideas that were extraordinarily influential, but rarely questioned. These false hypotheses tend to be **stricken** from the historical record because they are embarrassing, particularly if institutions that were aligned with these hypotheses still exist. For instance, the great Henry Ford—who perfected the assembly line and who was a giant in the automotive industry—was also a great admirer of, and a pen pal with, another great anti-Semite: Adolf Hitler.[1] Henry Ford received the Grand Cross of the German Eagle, the highest medal Nazi Germany could give to a non-German. However, you won't find this story in any Ford commercial; if something does not fit with the desired history narrative, it is conveniently altered until the desirable storyline is created. For this reason, the great frequency with which the biggest and most prestigious institutions have been wrong is underestimated enormously. It is therefore quite likely that many commonly held beliefs today are wrong; in fact it is easy to demonstrate that they are. There are many areas where the commonly held—and institutionally held—opinions are at odds with research in the area, and ERP is such an area. During my research I found some statements that amounted to: *"ERP must be beneficial because so many highly paid executives cannot be wrong."* However, couldn't the same statement be made about mortgage-backed securities and credit default swaps? AIG, Goldman Sachs and Bear Stearns love them; these companies are chock full of smart people, so how could they be wrong?

People who are well disposed toward ERP will most likely read this book (actually they will most likely **not** read it) and reject it out of hand; how can people agree with something that is counter to their financial benefit? Obviously, if a person consults in ERP, that person is going to be sold on ERP. Who would ever be so thick as to believe something that could negatively affect their pocketbook? If you are a partner at a large consulting company that implements ERP systems

---

[1] Yes, he perfected the assembly line. , Henry Ford was not the inventor of the assembly line as is commonly presented in business textbooks. http://www.scmfocus.com/productionplanningandscheduling/2012/07/04/who-was-the-first-to-engage-in-mass-production-ford-or-the-venetians/.

and your large house and large Lexus have been paid for by ERP implementations, you will not want to read this book—guaranteed—and you will not want other people to read it. Your life would be more difficult if this information got out. However, if you are one of these partners, the problem is that you will have nothing but anecdotal evidence (you have seen ERP work and provide value to clients), *argumentum ad numerum* (lots of companies use ERP and how can they be wrong?), or *ad hominem* (the author must not know what he or she is talking about)[2], because the research on ERP will not support what you are telling your clients nor your luxurious lifestyle.

Very few people have suggested what I propose in this book, so it's rare that people have even had to confront the question of the evaluation of evidence regarding the benefits of ERP. I can anticipate the negative responses because one person, Cynthia Rettig, wrote one of the few articles that were not critical of ERP in an ancillary way, but were critical of ERP's foundation. Many of the criticisms of her article fell into categories listed in the previous paragraph (argumentum ad numerum, ad hominem, etc.). Even the most educated part of society—people with PhDs in the sciences—finish their academic careers **still clinging to the idea** that new discoveries disproving the theories upon which they built their careers must somehow be wrong. A famous example of this is Albert Einstein. Einstein was eerily prescient about most of his scientific hypothesis; in fact he is widely credited with seeing fifty years beyond any of his contemporaries. However, when he made predictions about the new science of quantum mechanics, he was incorrect. Niels Bohr—a thought leader in what was an entirely new field and who did not follow rules of "large" physics—was proven correct. It turns out that God does play with dice after all.[3]

The desire to find evidence to support one's already existing hypothesis and to filter out contradictory information is called "confirmation bias." It is one of the

---

[2] See the section on logical fallacies, presented on page 8.

[3] For those who may not get the reference, Einstein and Bohr disagreed about the randomness of outcomes at the subatomic level. Bohr proposed, and was later proven to be true, that the outcomes are probabilistic. Einstein saw the universe as far more ordered than this, most likely because at the level of most of this research, it is. His famous quote on this topic was that, *"God does not play dice"* (that is, with the universe). But studies of the tiniest particles have shown a universe that is very strange, and laws from outside this domain are not particularly applicable.

most powerful of cognitive biases and exists in all of us—except not necessarily to the same degree in each individual, and not to the same degree in each individual at each age in their lifetime. Confirmation bias explains why things that are learned early in life, no matter how false, are adhered to so strongly into adulthood. It explains why advertisers will pay more to reach younger viewers than older viewers. The young brain is the most malleable; it exhibits what neurologists call neuroplasticity and as such it can learn new things quickly. As the brain ages, it develops specific neural connections (actually, the development of knowledge means creating some neural connections at the expense of other neural connections), meaning that it becomes increasingly "hard wired" for particular thoughts and particular ways of thinking as we age.

Although sometimes suggested, it is not true that the best-educated people are immune to confirmation bias. The more an individual has invested in any philosophy or course of action, the more they have to lose by adapting to a new way of thinking. In fact, merely following advice can reduce the ability to question that advice, particularly if that advice comes from an entity with some type of authority. The investment can be both **psychological** as well as **real** (in that one receives negative real world consequences for changing one's views). Both of these factors—the psychological need to protect previous mental investments as well as real world consequences of changing one's views—frequently combine to prevent people from changing to a new and better way of doing things and often make the mind impervious to contradictory information. There is research indicating that math is performed with less accuracy when the conclusion is in conflict with one's beliefs.[4]

One question to ask is: "Can the person who disagrees with the contentions in this book actually afford to agree with them?" Most importantly, do they have a financial bias? As for myself, I can reasonably propose that I am financially unbiased with respect to ERP, unlike the few other authors who have written on the topic of ERP. I do not make my income from ERP, but I do derive work based on the sale or implementation of ERP. I connect the systems I work with to ERP, and if ERP were to go away tomorrow, I would simply connect a different system to the planning systems in which I specialize. For the longest time it has been

---

[4] Motivated Numeracy and Enlightened Self-Government.

proposed that ERP serves as a backbone and helps the implementation of other systems. However, from my experience I have found that ERP tends to **interfere** with implementing other systems (although, I should say that all of my implementation experience is with "Big ERP," and in performing research for this book and other research initiatives at SCM Focus, I've found some ERP systems that do not impose as much interference). I have been impressed with several smaller "ERP" applications; while they have similarities in terms of their footprint; they have nothing in common with Tier 1 or Tier 1 ERP software vendors in terms of costs, account control, business model, and a variety of other factors. These are covered in the book, *Replacing ERP: Breaking the Big ERP Habit with Flexible Applications at a Fraction of the Cost.*

As I will explain several times throughout this book, since I began working with ERP in 1997, I have found that ERP systems have interfered with the value that can be obtained from business intelligence systems, bill of material systems, web storefronts, etc., in addition to the planning systems I have implemented (in fact, pretty much any system that must be connected to the ERP system). In the past I simply accepted this as the way it was: I thought IT implementation had to be difficult and frustrating. My exposure to many systems that are far easier to implement and have better functionality than Big ERP has led me to question my assumptions. More companies should be asking themselves this question; unfortunately these types of questions are not asked because a groupthink has settled over the topic of ERP.

Understanding the Philosophical Basis for ERP

ERP is based upon the oversimplified concept that companies should buy an integrated financial/manufacturing/supply chain/sales management system. This concept could be implemented well or poorly, but it is important to differentiate the implementation of the concept (that is the resulting software application) from the concept itself. Proponents of ERP state that the ERP concept is not only beneficial, but that ERP systems are a **requirement** for all companies. Companies that don't buy and implement ERP systems are "not with the times" and "don't have good executives making decisions for them." In fact, the logical fallacy used in promoting this concept is "appeal to fear," and it is effective against executive decision-makers who must keep marketable acronyms such as ERP on their resumes. For some time, being involved in or overseeing ERP implementations was an important addition to an executive's resume.

In the course of doing research for this book, I found a number of articles that implied that companies where ERP has not yet been implemented should absolutely be thinking of using an ERP system. These articles present **no evidence** that companies benefit from ERP, but instead rely upon the logical fallacy of *"argumentum ad numerum"*—that many companies have implemented ERP. They then combined this fallacy with **hypothetical** statements about how ERP software may benefit a company.[5] Furthermore, this viewpoint is not contradicted by the opposing viewpoint that ERP may not always be the best approach. There is little variability and very little independent thinking on the topic. Further on in this book, after a review of the research on ERP benefits has been presented, the reader should question whether this unanimity of opinion is justified.

Companies have invested an enormous number of resources into ERP systems, and contrary to the opinion presented in most of the literature in the area, the failings of ERP to meet the expectations of implementing companies is not something that can be rectified simply with a change in management practice or by hiring a new implementation consultant. This is because the aspects of ERP that have been most disappointing are related to the fact that the concept of ERP—regardless of the specific implementation of the concept (the software)—was never as advantageous as was presented. Once companies can interpret these limitations as permanent in nature, they can begin to deal with ERP in a realistic manner rather than by relying upon a new release, wishful thinking, or some new marketing construct provided by their ERP vendor to improve the condition of their ERP systems.

Clearly, information generally available on ERP systems is subject to financial bias, for the obvious reason that the ERP industry is so large and so lucrative. Just a few ERP implementations can make a partner at a large consulting company well off, as they make a lot of money off of their consultants and it takes many

---

[5] Many of these articles applied the logical fallacies of "wishful thinking" or "appeals to probability."

consultants to implement an ERP system.[6] For salespeople who sell ERP systems, the same rules apply. Because of the financial bias that exists, information published about ERP is quite positive, bordering on the Pollyannaish. Meanwhile, negative information about ERP tends to be suppressed. When negative information about ERP (mostly in the form of information about failed implementations) does get out, normally the information is **spun** so that the software and the **concept of ERP** is not blamed. Instead, the repetitive narrative is that the implementing company must have made some mistakes, and these mistakes are simply managerial in nature and therefore correctable.

Clearly, with all this money to be made in ERP systems, the question of who can be trusted to provide accurate information on ERP is clearly not a question that I have come up with exclusively, as the following quotation demonstrates.

> *"ERP is a multi-billion dollar industry dominated by consultants and software vendors. This is not going to change anytime soon since software and software expertise are the necessities of an automated system. But for a practitioner within an industry responsible for a project and a company that must live with the outcomes, the question is: Who solely has your best interest in mind? I can say only one thing: The deck is clearly stacked against you."* — Control Your ERP Destiny: Reduce Project Costs, Mitigate Risks, and Design Better Business Solutions

Financial bias has caused some highly inaccurate information to be released by most of those who have written about ERP. The fact that so many entities were spectacularly wrong with respect to their predictions for ERP has been one of the great missed stories of enterprise software. And who will cover this story? The IT

---

[6] Roughly two thirds of the hourly rate paid to Big ERP consultants goes not to the consultant but to the consulting company. However, most of the work is done by the consultant, not the consulting company and definitely not by the partner. The investment by consulting companies into the consultants is minimal—if they are junior they will be sent to software training. The entire structure of consulting companies is primarily about overcharging the "client" versus what is paid out in wages, and pushing that money up the food chain. The exploitation does not end when one makes partner because senior partners exploit partners. It is a highly unequal system—not based upon work or the value added by each individual—but based upon power.

press themselves are the main culprits; after all, will those who take in advertising revenue from ERP vendors break the story that the emperor has no clothes? It fits into the overall storyline of ERP systems; in fact, the ERP phenomenon cannot really be understood without understanding how wrong the projections about ERP have been, and therefore, this is a main theme of this book. It is only through understanding why these projections were so wrong and by taking a full account of ERP as it is today (not blindly accepting the fabricated sales pitch of entities that make their money from implementing ERP), that companies that already have ERP can determine the best way to manage ERP in the future. Secondly, for companies that have not yet implemented ERP, this book will address how to avoid the mistakes of companies that jumped on the ERP bandwagon to their great detriment, and are now stuck in a situation where the system is negatively impacting their ability to meet business requirements and ERP's resource consumption crowds out best-of-breed solutions.

Unintended Consequences and the Definition of Success

The promises to ERP buyers have not come true, but many things that ERP buyers were never promised and never expected—such as the power that enterprise software buyers handed over to ERP vendors after implementing ERP (and particularly Big ERP vendors and big consulting companies) or the large percentage of the IT budget that the ERP system would consume into perpetuity—did become realities. Therefore, it's quite important to differentiate between the commercial success of ERP and **the benefits analysis of what ERP does for companies**. No one could dispute that ERP has been tremendously successful for ERP software vendors and for the major consulting companies. On the basis of software sales, ERP systems comprise the highest grossing category of application software ever developed. The sales, implementation, and maintenance of ERP systems have created an enormous number of well-paying jobs and quite well off ERP salesmen and consulting firm partners. Currently all of the major consulting companies are dependent upon their ERP consulting practice to make their numbers. However, what this book will focus on is the value that ERP **provides to the companies that implement it**.

This book will address two major assumptions. The first is the unquestioned assumption that ERP is necessary. The second assumption is that Big ERP actually benefits companies. As this book will demonstrate, there is no evidence to support these views, and there is quite a bit of evidence that ERP has been an unfortunate misallocation of resources within enterprise software. (In fact, the evidence is that ERP is the largest misallocation of resources to have ever occurred in the history of enterprise software—possibly not as momentous a statement as it appears to be as the history of enterprise software only goes back to the early 1970s, but the total resources expended on ERP since its inception have been gigantic.) This book explains the background of ERP, the expectations that were set for it, and why it is a myth that ERP systems improve the state of companies better than other software that could be implemented. ERP proponents say it is "ERP versus **nothing**"—a logical fallacy called a "false dichotomy/false dilemma" that is used to stack the deck in favor or ERP—however, the question is really "ERP versus true alternative applications" and therefore alternative expenditures of resources.

The Consensus on ERP

In the previous section I discussed the commonly held belief that ERP is essential infrastructure for a company, something that is particularly true if the company in question is in manufacturing. It is interesting that Aberdeen Research wrote a paper that stated the following about this type of assumption right in the title of the paper:

> *"To ERP or Not to ERP: In Manufacturing, It Isn't Even a Question."*

The words in this title can be described reasonably as the general consensus on ERP, but it is a curious consensus considering ERP's history. Interestingly, one cannot find consulting advice that questions whether ERP is even a good idea. The only real topic of conversation is when to implement ERP software or **how to improve ERP implementations**. If one does not have ERP installed, the question is not whether ERP is a good fit, a good value, and can meet the company's business requirements, but why ERP hasn't been implemented already and when the company plans to implement it. Therefore, for the most part, Aberdeen's research conclusion is correct: this is what the majority of manufacturers believe. But what Aberdeen does not know is that this assumption is not true. With this consensus about ERP among those who provide advice, it is little wonder that most enterprise software buyers believe they need ERP as explained in the quotations below:

> *"More than 85 percent of respondents agreed or strongly agreed that their ERP systems were essential to the core of their businesses, and that they 'could not live without them.' Interestingly, just 4 percent of IT leaders said their ERP system offered their companies competitive differentiation or advantage."* — Thomas Wailgun, CIO

> *"'The business sees the slick demos and possibilities, and then keeps forking over the money for this, and they don't understand why they are still paying all this money,' Wang says. 'Why is it so hard to get a simple report? Why is it so hard to add a new product or build a new product line? Why is it so hard to get <u>consolidated financial information</u>? [underline added] Isn't that the whole point of ERP?'"* — Thomas Wailgun, CIO

Companies see the low functionality and the poor reporting functionality of their ERP systems, along with the problems integrating with non-ERP systems, but they don't seem to be able to put the separate data points together into a complete story. As "everybody" has implemented and used ERP, how could ERP itself be bad?

Books and Other Publications on Software Selection

I perform a comprehensive literature review before I begin writing any book. One of my favorite quotations about research is from the highly respected RAND Corporation, a think tank based in Santa Monica, California—a location not far from where I grew up and where I used to walk with my friend when I was in high school—at that time having no idea of the historically significant institution that I would stroll by on my lost surfing weekends. RAND's *Standards for High Quality Research and Analysis* publication makes the following statement regarding how its research references other work.

> *"A high-quality study cannot be done in intellectual isolation: it necessarily builds on and contributes to a body of research and analysis. The relationships between a given study and its predecessors should*

be rich and explicit. The study team's understanding of past research should be evident in many aspects of its work, from the way in which the problem is formulated and approached to the discussion of the findings and their implications. The team should take particular care to explain the ways in which its study agrees, disagrees, or otherwise differs importantly from previous studies. Failure to demonstrate an understanding of previous research lowers the perceived quality of a study, despite any other good characteristics it may possess."

There are so many books that promote ERP, rather than analyze ERP, that there was little to reference when doing research for this book—this is a "why" book rather than a "how" book. **Books on ERP have a strong tendency to deal in platitudes and unexamined assumptions,** and offer very little new or different information on the topic. The closest I could find to a book that applied some critical thinking to ERP was, *Control Your ERP Destiny: Reduce Project Costs, Mitigate Risks, and Design Better Business Solutions*, which is sort of a "tell all" book about the errors of ERP implementations. However, as with almost all ERP books, it concentrates on providing information to companies to help improve their ERP implementations rather than questioning the logical and evidentiary foundation for ERP.

Most of the references in this book you are reading are not from other books, but from a combination of my personal experience and some articles (including academic articles) that study the impacts and benefits of ERP. The only quality ERP statistics came from either academic research or, to far a lesser degree, IT analysts. And very little of the material from ERP vendors was found to be reliable; even when they point out flaws in the arguments of other ERP vendors, they proceed to promote their own arguments, which are not based on evidence and often contain logical fallacies. Smaller ERP vendors have gone on the aggressive against Big ERP abuses, but often their arguments are also self-serving. And after reviewing a number of ERP applications, some of the best smaller ERP systems are certainly not the loudest nor do they have the biggest marketing budgets. Some might say that this should be obvious, as these are software vendors and thus entirely biased. However, this has not been true of all vendors in all software categories that I have analyzed. For example, some vendors in the other software categories covered by SCM Focus have added significant content to their space. One vendor that has provided very good and very accurate content in the area of ERP is e2b enterprise, and they are referenced throughout this book.[7, 8]

Many of the authors who work for both IT analyst firms as well as IT periodicals frequently quote statistics from other sources, with the same statistics referenced repeatedly. Some of the conclusions that were drawn from the research of others display clear logical errors. Many authors in this area are simply not qualified or have not spent the time to try to make sense of the numbers and to triangulate them with other sources. They may be effective beat reporters, but they lack a background in research. Because of this, one finds that many of the same numbers are repeated in various articles; however, when you study the underlying research, you will find that the conclusions do not follow from the statistic that is quoted in the secondarily sourced article. Executive decision makers certainly do not have time to perform this type of analysis themselves, and as a result, there is little doubt that many of them have been misled by authors who lacked the background to perform the analysis for the articles that they wrote on ERP.

The most prolific IT analyst firm with respect to ERP cost estimation is Aberdeen. However, Aberdeen's cost estimates are not realistic. They greatly underestimate the implementation costs for ERP projects, as well as underestimate the variance in license costs between the Tier 1 and Tier 2 vendors (projecting them with an average cost per user no greater than 15 percent in a study that included SAP, Oracle, Lawson and QAD). Aberdeen did, however, have an interesting estimate of the average number of users per ERP vendor, and that helped reinforce how various ERP vendors tend to sell into different sized companies. This is well known in the industry, but the exact figures helped drive the point home.

One of the more comprehensive studies of the benefits of ERP also evaluated the research on ERP, and explained their findings in the following quotation.

---

[7] This is not a commentary on the value provided by the Tier 2 ERP vendors—it is simply a rating of the usability of their content.

[8] And most of this work is from James Mallory, their Business Connections Officer.

"Previous evidence on ERP systems has come from qualitative case studies (e.g., Markus et al. 2000) or surveys of self-reported perceptual performance (e.g., Swanson and Wang 2003), but relatively few studies collect data from a large number of firms or use objective measures of productivity and performance." — Which Came First, IT or Productivity?

This lack of information also demonstrates that the demand for such information was never very high. ERP was one of the most powerful trends in enterprise software; however, it was one that was driven largely without the support of academic or other forms of research. This may have been attributed to the compelling logic of ERP. Some philosophies have their own appeal and lower the need for proof in order to make people believe them to be true. ERP was clearly one of these philosophies.

I cannot explain why so much writing on the topic of ERP is so generic and duplicated, I only know that this is what I found. In performing research for this book, I would frequently jump between different books and articles; often the similarities were so striking that it seemed as if I were reading from the same book or article.

What Type of ERP Is This Book Focused On?

There is a confusing aspect to ERP software in that ERP is both a category of software, as well as a way of doing business. This book is focused on the history of ERP: primarily large ERP software vendors following an on-premises model. However, there is another modality of ERP: the integrated software approach is used, but ERP is not used as a wedge through which to control the account or to sell in mediocre non-ERP applications. Best described as "small software vendor ERP," it does not match the predominant model that I spend most of the book describing—this book is about the predominant forms of ERP that have been practiced up to the point of this book's publication, which is software from Tier 1 and Tier 2 ERP software vendors. It should be understood that small vendor (SaaS-based solutions, open source, etc.) ERP has had a very small impact on the overall ERP market. Therefore, I do not want to paint all ERP systems and modalities or operations with the same brush.

The Book's Scientific Method Orientation

Typically books about ERP are not based on any evidence, but instead describe how to implement ERP better or faster—sometimes from an experiential perspective, but also from a purely hypothetical perspective. This book is different. It uncovers the realities of ERP—not simply what ERP was predicted to do, or sunny sales observations of what it could do hypothetically. Instead, it uses academic research combined with my consulting experience to explain what companies have acquired from ERP and what can be expected from ERP in the future. Essentially, the standard way an ERP book is written is to work backward from what vendors have proposed to be true about ERP, or what authors would like to be true about ERP, rather than what is proven about ERP. Most authors in the ERP area make their living from ERP, and so have little interest in doing anything but promoting ERP and furthering their career. ERP is now more than thirty years old; readers of this book should attempt to resist suggestions of a "change of course"—the proposal that while something has been bad in the past, this bad thing (whatever that thing is) no long applies because "it's a new day." In fact, the story on ERP—and even the story on ERP applications themselves—has not changed very much in the past decade. Change of course is essentially an argumentative technique that seeks to extinguish the analysis of history, which is inconvenient and interferes with the proposed future that another person would prefer to be the accepted assumption.

Tilting at Windmills

ERP is utterly dominant in the enterprise software space "right or wrong," so why write a book, that takes a clear-eyed appraisal of ERP? What possible good could come of such an analysis?

Contrary to popular belief, not all companies have implemented ERP. Given the evidence in this book, is there is any reason for those companies that do not use ERP to start? Furthermore, many companies that have ERP systems have implemented only certain modules, and within these modules only certain functionality. Perhaps by communicating the true payoff of ERP, this book will have a positive effect by making even small adjustments in the behavior and decision-making of ERP vendors and buying companies. ERP vendors and consulting companies that specialize in ERP have not given their clients the accurate story. That is a problem because every year, companies must essentially decide anew how much to reinvest in their ERP system. This reinvestment can take many forms.

1. *Support Fees and Upgrades:* Means paying the yearly support fee, and upgrading the software—which also means investing resources in understanding the release notes, testing the new version—making sure the new version is compatible with other applications and with already written customizations.

2. *Deepening the use of ERP:* Often means choosing to activate more ERP modules and more functionality within the modules as well as adding more customization to the system to meet various business requirements.

3. *Adding More Non-ERP Applications from the ERP Vendor:* Can mean purchasing additional non-ERP applications from their ERP vendor that will not necessarily give the business what they need but will meet the needs of the IT department and will be "integrated" to their ERP system. This can extend to infrastructure, content management and business intelligence software. Some of the large ERP vendors in particular develop sales plans to take over most of the software purchase for **any** enterprise software that their current ERP customers buy.

4. *Deepening the Interaction with the Vendor:* Software vendors like their customers to attend conferences, talk about their success stories, be part of user groups, etc.

The most common decision over the past several decades has been for companies with ERP systems to **increase** their involvement and purchases with their ERP vendor in any of the ways mentioned above, but is that the right decision? Purchasing companies get a steady stream of information from the software vendor and consulting companies that other customers who follow the advice that the ERP vendor recommends continue to see gains in their business and efficiency—but is this true? So much of this information is financially biased because it comes from a desire to sell more ERP software and services, but where can companies turn to find out the "real story," and one that is not biased by promotion.[9] After you complete this book you will have a much better idea as to whether it is or is not.

My Background and the Book's Focus and Orientation

It's important to talk about my background. I am an author and independent consultant, and I spent my career working in supply chain planning software. My career has provided me with exposure to not only supply chain software, but also to ERP, reporting, middleware and infrastructure software. I, like the rest of the IT industry, tended to accept ERP systems as a standard. ERP systems were the mother ship to which all other applications connected. When I first began working with ERP back in 1997, I was certified in the SAP ERP Sales and Distribution (SD) module. Back then I had no idea what module to specialize in. Some partner at KPMG looked at my supply chain education and two years of consulting experience and put me onto the Materials Management module training track. I found the training so tedious that after a week I transferred into the Sales and Distribution module and became a certified SD consultant. However, SD proved to be just as tedious as materials management. After five or so months doing things like creating and testing sales orders, I left for i2 Technologies, which at that time was a thought leader in supply chain planning. After hearing so much about how ERP was taking over the world, and how great its supply chain functionality was, I was extremely disappointed to find that the functionality contained in SAP ERP was so elementary. For years I specialized in integrating advanced planning systems to SAP ERP, and on nearly every project I had to account for how the systems that I worked with integrated to SAP ERP—sometimes from the data perspective and sometimes from the process perspective. Therefore, over the years I have accumulated a great deal of exposure to ERP systems and to the systems that connect to ERP. I have also worked in a wide variety of roles, from junior configuration consultant to integration lead, to functional lead, solution architect and system analyst, and even occasionally as a project manager. I have

---

[9] Some may think that the IT analysts or the major IT publications may fill this role, but in actuality most IT analysts are aligned with ERP vendors. That is they are producer- rather than consumer-oriented in their editorial content. For those interested in the influence of software vendors over IT analysts, the SCM Focus Press book, *Gartner and the Magic Quadrant: A Guide for Buyers, Vendors, Investors* explains this in detail.

written on a wide variety of supply chain software topics, with my first articles appearing in 2003. My areas of interest extend from documenting the configuration of systems to IT strategy.

The Book's Applicability to SaaS and On-premises ERP Vendors

This book is about on-premises ERP. On-premises software is the traditional enterprise software model where the software is taken by the implementing company after purchase and installed on the company's servers, rather than the model where the software is "rented" and the software vendor hosts the software. The on-premises model is presently the dominant form of ERP software, and of course, has been since ERP was first introduced. However, many vendors provide SaaS or cloud-based ERP, and they use the term ERP even though their solutions are more limited in scope than on-premises ERP. This is not necessarily a bad thing, but it does confuse the issue somewhat when I want to use the term ERP; any number of SaaS-based ERP vendors could say that the conclusions in this book do not apply to them, and they would be right. SaaS vendors don't have the same ability to lock in customers as do on-premises vendors. They are still relatively new and do not have the same history as on-premises ERP solutions, so it cannot be expected that the research I will quote will apply to them. In addition, my project experience is 100 percent with on-premises solutions, so when it comes to SaaS ERP, I do not have the same personal experience upon which to draw. SaaS solutions currently represent about 4 percent of all enterprise software sales, but because the software is less expensive, this represents a higher percentage of "seats" served than this 4 percent value would indicate. One of the more interesting topics is how SaaS ERP systems will alter the ERP landscape, but I intend to cover that topic as part of the SCM Focus Press book, *Replacing ERP: Breaking the Big ERP Habit with Flexible Applications at a Fraction of the Cost.*

The Vendors Covered in This Book

The largest ERP vendors in the world are SAP, Oracle, Microsoft, Infor and Epicor. SAP and Oracle are considered Tier 1 ERP vendors, while Microsoft, Infor and Epicor are considered Tier 2. However, because I work with SAP software, most of the examples in this book are from SAP. The Tier 1 market is dominated by SAP and Oracle, and many of the statements regarding SAP generalize to Oracle as well as to Tier 2 ERP vendors. There are also a variety of vendors that are neither Tier 1 nor Tier 2, but which are provide some ERP functionality, but do not follow the business strategies of the major ERP vendors, and I discuss these vendors as well. Additionally, non-ERP vendors are described in this book to illustrate various principles.

How Writing Bias Is Controlled at SCM Focus and SCM Focus Press

Bias is a serious problem in the enterprise software field. Large vendors receive uncritical coverage of their products, and large consulting companies recommend the large vendors that have the resources to hire and pay consultants rather than the vendors with the best software for the client's needs.

At SCM Focus, we have yet to financially benefit from a company's decision to buy an application showcased in print, either in a book or on the SCM Focus website. This may change in the future as SCM Focus grows—but we have been writing with a strong viewpoint for years without coming into any conflicts of interest. SCM Focus has the most stringent rules related to controlling bias and restricting commercial influence of any information provider. These "writing rules" are provided in the link below:

http://www.scmfocus.com/writing-rules/

If other information providers followed these rules, we would be able to learn about software without being required to perform our own research and testing for every topic.

Information about enterprise supply chain planning software can be found on the Internet, but this information is primarily promotional or written at such a high level that none of the important details or limitations of the application are exposed; this is true of books as well. When only one enterprise software application is covered in a book, one will find that the application works perfectly; the application operates as expected and there are no problems during the implementation to bring the application live. This is all quite amazing and quite different from my experience of implementing enterprise software. However, it is very difficult to make a living by providing objective information about enterprise supply chain software, especially as it means being critical at some point. I once remarked to a friend that SCM Focus had very little competition in providing untarnished information on this software category, and he said, "Of course, there is no money in it."

The Approach to the Book

By writing this book, I wanted to help people get exactly the information they need without having to read a lengthy volume. The approach to the book is essentially the same as to my previous books, and in writing this book I followed the same principles.

1. *Be direct and concise.* There is very little theory in this book and the math that I cover is simple. This book is focused on software and for most users and implementers of the software the most important thing to understand is conceptually what the software is doing.

2. *Based on project experience.* Nothing in the book is hypothetical; I have worked with it or tested it on an actual project. My project experience has led to my understanding a number of things that are not covered in typical supply planning books. In this book, I pass on this understanding to you.

The SCM Focus Site

As I am also the author of the SCM Focus site, http://www.scmfocus.com, the site and the book share a number of concepts and graphics. Furthermore, this book contains many links to articles on the site, which provide more detail on specific subjects.

Intended Audience

This book should be of interest to anyone who wishes to learn whether ERP actually provides the intended benefits, to learn about the history of ERP systems, and to learn how information systems are marketed to companies and how that information is interpreted by software buyers. However, the reader who will find this information most valuable is the one who needs help determining their company's overall enterprise software strategy.

If you have any questions or comments on the book, please e-mail me at shaunsnapp@scmfocus.com.

Abbreviations

A listing of all abbreviations used throughout the book is provided at the end of the book.

Corrections

Corrections and updates, as well as reader comments, can be viewed in the comment section of this book's web page. Also, if you have comments or questions, please add them to the following link:

http://www.scmfocus.com/scmfocuspress/it-decision-making-books/the-real-story-behind-erp/

CHAPTER 2

The History of ERP

I find it amazing that there is so little information about the history of ERP, other than a few short articles on the Internet and the paper *ERP: A Short History*, by F. Robert Jacobs and F.C. Weston Jr. in 2007 in the *Journal of Operations Management.* It is curious, but I can come to no other conclusion than this: very rarely have ERP systems been put under the microscope. The articles on ERP tend to accept all of the initial proposed benefits of ERP as if they were true, and almost all of the materials written about ERP systems since ERP systems were first introduced (outside of academic materials) have been promotional in nature. The articles have not demonstrated historical knowledge and certainly are not scientific in their orientation (that is, based on evidence and/or testing). Book after book, and article after article, promote ERP and provide advice about improving ERP implementations—yet never do the authors question the benefits of ERP. The influence of ERP has been so great and has so strongly impacted the structure of the enterprise software market (in addition to impacting the decisions that are made by companies outside decisions about ERP itself), that ERP as a topic really deserves a comprehensive written history. What follows is not that comprehensive history by any means, but enough of a background to support the analysis presented in the following chapters.

What is ERP?

Conceptually, ERP is a combined set of modules that share a database and user interface, and that supports multiple functions used by different business units.[10] Because the ERP modules use a single database, employees in different divisions (e.g., accounting and sales) can rely on the same information for their specific needs and without any time lag. ERP covers what are sometimes considered a company's "core" business processes. These processes are mirrored in the four basic modules of SAP's ERP system:

- Sales and Distribution

- Materials Management

- Production Planning

- Financial and Controlling

ERP Gets its Start

A bill of materials (BOM) is the listing of components and subcomponents that make up a finished good. The first enterprise system in which the BOM was encapsulated was the material requirements planning system, or MRP system for short. Major MRP functionality is shown in the following graphic.

---

[10] The ERP system is on a single database if the ERP implementation is a **single instance,** which is not always the case, as is explained in Chapter 6: "Analyzing the Logic Used to Sell ERP."

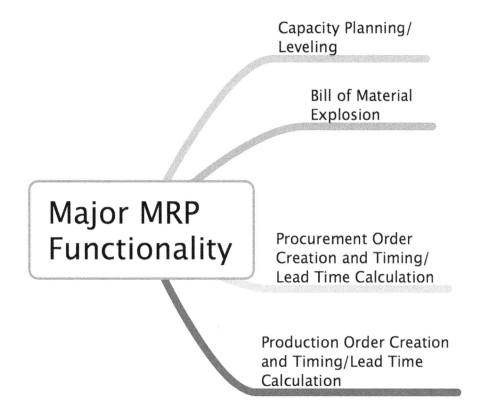

I will use the term "MRP" a number of times in this book, and you may notice that MRP sounds very similar to the term "ERP." This is not a coincidence; ERP is actually based upon the term MRP, although as we will see, it is not a particularly descriptive term for what ERP actually does.[11]

MRP software predated ERP software by more than a decade, with MRP systems beginning to be implemented in the mid 1970s and ERP systems beginning to be implemented in the mid 1980s. At one time, MRP systems were sold as standalone systems, and there were around thirty competitors in the market. Many ERP vendors acquired MRP vendors and began to include this software as part of a broader integrated offering. In its earliest incarnation, ERP software was known as "business systems" software. Prior to the change in terminology, vendors of business systems were simply growing the footprint of their applications; it was

---

[11] The MRP planning method is actually contained within ERP systems.

actually the IT analyst firm Gartner that began referring to these systems as Enterprise Resource Planning, or ERP. However, as previously stated, in time the MRP software vendors became subsumed within ERP suites primarily through mergers and acquisitions.

> *"In the early 1980s, MRP expanded from a material planning and control system to a company-wide system capable of planning and controlling virtually all of the firm's resources. This expanded approach was so fundamentally different from the original concept of MRP that Wight (1984) coined the term MRP II, which refers to manufacturing resource planning. A major purpose of MRP II is to integrate primary functions (i.e., production, marketing and finance) and other functions such as personnel, engineering, and purchasing into the planning process.*
>
> *"A key difference between MRP II and ERP is that while MRP II has traditionally focused on the planning and scheduling of internal resources, ERP strives to plan and schedule supplier resources as well, based on the dynamic customer demands and schedules."*
> — Planning for ERP Systems: Analysis and Future Trend

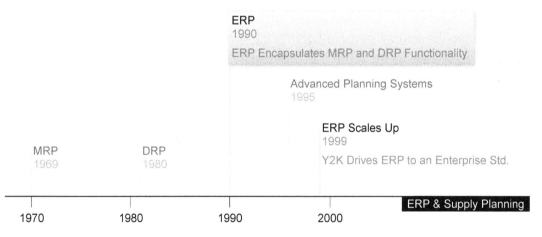

The dates in the above chart are estimates of when these technologies became broadly used, not when they were first developed.

MRP is a method of performing supply and production planning. MRP is quite simple and requires nothing more than elementary arithmetic to perform its functions.[12] The software processing requirements are quite low. For instance, while a supply and production planning problem will take hours to run using more advanced methods, MRP can be run for the entire supply network in just a few minutes.

Even two decades after the rise of advanced supply chain planning software, MRP is still the dominant procedure/method used in companies around the world for supply and demand planning. MRP is also run in external supply chain planning applications; however, the vast majority of MRP planning runs that are performed today are performed in ERP systems. Let us look at two graphics that succinctly explain how MRP works.

MRP for Manufacturing Items

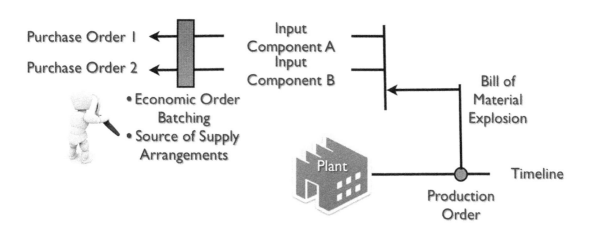

For procured items, MRP converts forecasts and sales orders into purchase orders and production orders with the right dates so material can be brought in on time

---

[12] Today there are now a number of more advanced methods such as heuristics and cost optimization. However, MRP was the first to be broadly purchased as a commercial application. I cover the topic of MRP in my book, *Supply Planning in MRP, DRP and APS Software*. MRP was the first computerized procedure for supply and production planning, and it was the dominant procedure for some time.

to support demand. Additionally, the purchase orders and production orders are batched (that is, they are not necessarily in the same quantities as the sales orders) in order to meet order minimums and to create economic order quantities.

MRP for Procured Items

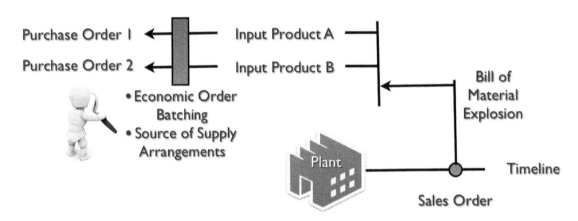

Both MRP for procured items and MRP for manufactured items are inbound methods. There is also a method for outbound planning, which is called DRP (distribution requirements planning. I won't get into DRP here, but I do explain the history of it in the article below:

http://www.scmfocus.com/scmhistory/2012/08/the-history-of-mrp-and-drp/

The Focus of ERP Systems
The relationship between MRP and ERP systems that I have described up to this point could easily lead one to believe that ERP systems were first designed to meet the needs of supply chain management. However, the opposite is true. In fact, ERP systems were actually designed to first meet the needs of finance and sales, and to a lesser degree, manufacturing and supply chain management. When one compares the functionality depth in the SAP ERP modules of Sales and Distribution (SD), Material Management (MM), Production Planning (PP), and Finance and Controlling (FI/CO), FI/CO has by far the greatest depth in functionality.

The major selling point of ERP systems was not that these systems provided particularly good functionality in any operational area. In actuality, they provided very basic functionality in all areas (I will address the notion of best practices in Chapter 4: "The Best Practice Logic for ERP"), but anything that occurred in operations was immediately reflected on the accounting side because all of the applications shared the same database. It was an argument tailor-made for executives: they would never have to personally deal with the functionality limitations of ERP systems. That is the common issue when the individuals who buy items are different from the individuals who use the item. Anyone who has had to use a centrally purchased corporate laptop should have no problem understanding this. However, as we will see further on, companies eventually paid for accepting the assumption that functionality did **not really matter** all that much, as long as all the applications were integrated.

Why Are ERP Systems Called ERP?

The first system that is recognized to be ERP was an enlargement of an MRP system. This was the IBM MMAS system. However, in an interesting historical turn of events, IBM never became a major player in the ERP space even though they had the first ERP system.[13]

> *"In 1975 IBM offered its Manufacturing Management and Account System (MMAS) which Bill Robinson from IBM considers a true precursor to ERP. It created general ledger postings and job costing plus forecasting updates emanating from both inventory and production transactions and could generate manufacturing orders from customer orders using either a standard bill of material or a bill of material attached to the customer order."* — ERP: A Short History

Gartner is credited with naming ERP systems. The term "ERP"—Enterprise Resource Planning—was adopted from the term "material requirements planning" (MRP) or "manufacturing requirements planning" by simply replacing the "M"

---

[13] Apparently, IBM was positioned to be a major vendor in the ERP space, in the same way they were positioned in the personal computing space, and let both markets slip through their fingers. However, I would not feel too bad for IBM, as they have done all right.

with an "E."[14] This was done because, in addition to containing the MRP supply and production planning method, ERP systems also contained sales, financial-accounting, and materials management functionality. Gartner found itself analyzing what appeared to be a new software category, and they needed a way to broaden out the terminology in a way that was more descriptive than "business systems." Additions to the MRP functionality made the application include more than just material or manufacturing, and expanded it to the entire "enterprise."[15]

ERP Begins Its Life with an Illogical Name

I was unable to find whom at Gartner actually named ERP. The term, although wildly successful, unfortunately is also inaccurate. Naming ERP systems after MRP made little sense because MRP is just one small component of what ERP does. Furthermore, ERP systems have little in the way of **actual planning functionality,** and instead are transaction processing systems. They are designed to do things like accept sales orders, create purchase requisitions and convert them to purchase orders, and then connect every transaction to the financial module. If anything, ERP systems were and continue to be the exact opposite of planning. ERP systems are generally known as "execution" systems. This is one reason why companies, after completing their ERP implementations, connected external supply chain planning applications to ERP to replace ERP's limited planning functionality. On the finance side, "planning" is not performed in the ERP system. Instead the data is exported to a flat file and opened in a spreadsheet or exported to a reporting application. Regardless of the area in which the analysis is performed, the best way to actually perform planning is to export the data from the ERP

---

[14] Manufacturing requirements planning (a.k.a. MRP II) was an extension of MRP that offered more functionality; therefore, in essence MRP II was another stepping stone on the way to ERP. There are several books on MRP II, but now this term is used very rarely in industry.

[15] "Enterprise" is a term I use quite a bit myself, but in fact, in this context it does not mean anything more than an organization. Therefore, linguistically, ERP would be identical to ORP. Perhaps enterprise sounds catchier than organization. There is an interesting insight on this term from the paper *Enterprise Resources Planning: Multisite ERP Implementations.—"The 'E' in ERP stands for 'enterprise.' But what exactly is an enterprise? A manufacturing plant composed of multiple cost centers? A business unit with profit and loss responsibility? A collection of business operations in a single geographic location? A legal entity? An entire corporation consisting of multiple business units and legal entities? The ambiguous definition of 'enterprise' means that complex organizations may implement enterprise systems in ways that do not really integrate the data and the process of the entire enterprise. Indeed, our research suggests that truly enterprise-wide implementations of ERP systems in large, complex organizations are the exception rather than the norm."*

system. In reality, ERP systems just tell companies **what already happened,** for use in planning for the future.

ERP Limitations

Companies found that planning was only the beginning of ERP's limitations. ERP is now well known for many limitations in its ability to present analytical data to customers. The shortcomings of ERP in this regard are a strong precursor to the growth of the separate business intelligence market, a market that was not supposed to have developed if the original projections by proponents of ERP had come true—that all reporting would be done within the ERP system. What was once known as "reporting" was renamed "business intelligence" to make it sound more appealing and leading edge. After all, "reporting" is boring...but "business intelligence" is leading edge. Business intelligence requires data to be extracted from ERP systems and placed into business intelligence repositories, and performs the reporting from these off-line repositories.[16]

This point is reinforced by the following quotation from Craig Sullivan of NetSuite, a vendor of SaaS ERP and other things.

> *"Stone-Age ERP was designed when businesses were top-heavy in general administration—when it was standard practice to have someone assigned to rekeying purchase orders or time and expense entries. Today, any unnecessary bureaucracy just wastes time that could be better spent elsewhere."*

Most ERP systems have not evolved past their humble roots, and to the disappointment of many companies that own ERP systems, many ERP systems have essentially stabilized. Stabilization is a development term that means only minimal improvements are being made to the system, as explained in the following quotation.

---

[16] There is a lot more to this topic, such as the hardware and software configuration of the data repositories and how frequently they are updated from the transaction system—all of which are covered in books on reporting/business intelligence. SCM Focus covers this topic at this sub-site: http://www.scmfocus.com/scmbusinessintelligence/.

"Our point is that current ERP technology provides an information-rich environment that is ripe for very intelligent planning and execution logic, yet little has changed since the late 1970s in the logic associated with such applications as forecasting, reorder point logic, MRP, production scheduling, etc. The current systems are now just executing the old logic much faster and in real-time. The area is ripe for innovative new approaches to these old problems. This may include partnering with our business counterparts who live in this dynamic environment on a day-to-day basis." — ERP: A Short History

The Implementation Success and Failure History of ERP

This book is about uncovering new information and synthesizing new observations from research performed previously. However, the historical problems with ERP systems have been very well advertised, and have been the subject of innumerable books and articles about how to improve the poor implementation success ratio of ERP systems. These articles maintain a consistent theme and seem to follow an algorithm.

1. *The Case Study:* Some company wasted an enormous amount of money on ERP.

2. *What to Improve:* The central concept to ERP is never questioned. Instead, the author moves onto an account of the management flaws that were at the root of the problem.

3. *The Solution:* The end of the article points out that it is important to obtain "top management support" when implementing ERP, and that companies need to change their business processes.

Following the algorithm analogy, the content of these articles could be programmed into a computer and generated automatically, with the company and the management flaw entered as variables, thus saving the author the time of having to manually write the article. Those working in the field certainly know that ERP implementations are so problematic, and I don't think I need to spend much time covering this well-established fact. However, I did find the following quotation to be educational.

"The preponderance of corporate pain lurking throughout the lifespan of a traditional on-premise ERP suite is unequivocal. To wit: ERP projects have only a 7 percent chance of coming in on time, most certainly will cost more than estimated, and very likely will deliver very unsatisfying results. In addition, today's enterprise has little better than a 50 percent chance that users will want to and actually use the application. Poor application design just adds to the turmoil. In sum, 'ERP success' has become a very subjective metric." — Why ERP Is Still So Hard

Only rarely is the actual success rate of ERP implementations quoted. According to the publication, *The Critical Success Factors for ERP Implementation: An Organizational Fit Perspective*, the success rate is roughly 25 percent. So, according to this source, 75 percent of ERP implementations are considered failures. But quoting just one study is misleading because the estimates are truly all over the map, as the quotation below attests.

"A study by the Standish Group estimates that 31 percent of projects are not successful (Kamhawi, 2007). Barker and Frolick (2003) suggest that 50 percent of ERP implementations are failures. Hong and Kim (2002) estimate a 75 percent failure rate, while Scott and Vessey (2002) estimates failure rates as high as 90 percent. Different statistics for the success or failure of ERP projects have been offered by researchers. In addition Bradford and Sandy (2002) reported that 57 percent of the companies they interviewed had not attempted to assess the performance of their ERP systems owing to a lack of empirically effective evaluation models." — Measures of Success in Project Implementing Enterprise Resource Planning

One of the most ridiculous arguments I've heard is that ERP implementations are so difficult that companies that manage to pull them off gain a competitive advantage over other companies. In this incarnation, the ERP system is presented as something akin to the Ironman Triathlon where the implementing company proves its toughness by running the gauntlet. It is an interesting analogy, which as far as I am aware is unique in the field of enterprise software where ease of implementation—rather than difficulty of implementation—is considered a virtue. And in fact, the argument is edging extremely close to circular reasoning: ERP is virtuous because it is difficult to do, and it is difficult to do because it is virtuous. It is also one of the few times that a high failure rate is presented as a positive attribute of a software category.

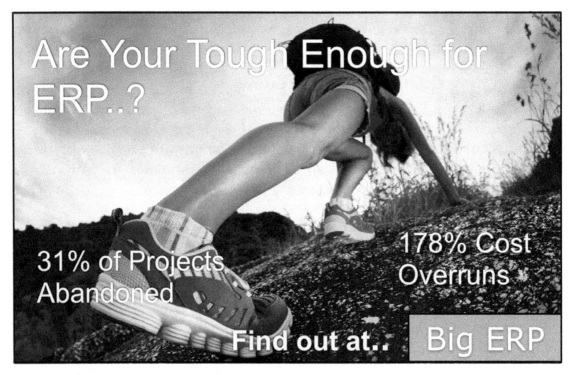

One can imagine airport advertisements like this, which focus on ERP's character-building qualities rather than on its negligible benefits.

What is interesting about the problematic implementation record of ERP is that it never seemed to quell the insatiable desire of companies to continue to implement ERP systems. This is the main takeaway: ERP was so quickly established as a **mandatory** application suite that not even gruesome stories of ERP failures and cost overruns could mitigate the desire for ERP implementations.

Discussed much less frequently is how effective ERP systems are in helping companies achieve their objectives after the systems are live. It turns out that the satisfaction level with ERP systems is low.

> *"Pretty much no one is really satisfied with the state of their ERP. Only 23 percent of users would recommend their ERP system to another enterprise. The truth is that ERP has been placed on the backburner because of the recession and manufacturers have suffered because of it."* — Old and Bad All Over Manufacturing

My research into ERP continually reinforced a central concept: very rarely does ERP impress the companies where it is installed. Instead, ERP tends to be discussed in terms of being a rite of passage. ERP is also commonly referred to as a "standard." But the adjective "good" does not seem to surface much in discussions about ERP systems. Of the ERP systems that I have worked with—and these systems are the more popular systems—I would say that none of them have impressed me. Furthermore, multiple aspects of the ERP system displease companies; common complaints include the following:

1. *Stagnant Applications:* There is a perceived lack of innovation on the part of ERP vendors. It is increasingly apparent that many ERP vendors are funneling their support revenues into other applications, leaving their existing ERP customers with dated applications.

2. *Costs:* ERP buyers frequently mention high costs of upgrades and support.[17]

3. *ERP Inflexibility:* The inability of ERP systems to be adjusted is a constant constraint that companies must work within.

---

[17] It is widely acknowledged that the Big ERP vendors make very high margins on their support contracts, as explained in the following quotation.

> *"There are strong economic drivers behind the move to third-party maintenance,' says Scavo. 'The OEM vendors are charging high amounts for their ongoing support. If you look at the financials of SAP and Oracle, you see that they realize very high margins on that and in many cases, the value of those services are not up to the price that customers are paying."* — Enterprise Apps Today

4. *Missing Required Functionality:* The inability of ERP to meet a company's business requirements, which leads to the following point.

5. *Customization:* There is constant need to customize the ERP system, leading to another complaint: the expense to upgrade ERP systems.

In a properly functioning media system, these types of issues would be the topic of more articles and better explained. Readers should ask: If ERP software vendors and consulting companies made all of these projections for how ERP would help companies, at some point shouldn't an investigation into the **actual benefits** of the software category be performed, particularly when it is the largest enterprise software category? Whose interests do the IT media support: the software vendors or the buyers? The IT media was instrumental in building up demand for ERP software and in serving as an echo chamber for software vendors and IT consultancies.

ERP and Account Control

The history papers that I reviewed for this book left out the fact that ERP was yet another attempt (and one of the most successful attempts by software vendors in the enterprise software space) to take control of clients. Each vendor replaced many of their client's applications with ERP, and then used their leverage as the ERP provider to sell more applications to these semi-captive companies. Mediocre systems were justified on the basis that they were at least integrated, and that having poor functionality in an integrated system was better than a nonintegrated system that provided the business with the functionality they needed to get their job done.

ERP had a second impact in that several vendors became extremely well positioned to sell other types of software. Two of the most powerful vendors were created through the ERP boom. One was SAP, which is the most successful ERP company and which parlayed this success into other enterprise software areas. Currently SAP stands as the largest enterprise software vendor in the world, and the second is Oracle, which extended its reach from the database into the application software realm with ERP software. From their dominant position in ERP, these vendors acquired a number of software companies that were effective at growing the company (although usually bad for the acquired software itself, as well as for the customers). SAP and Oracle have ridden the "ERP wave" and owe much of their current central position with customers to their role as the provider of the customers' ERP system.

Conclusion

Despite the enormous influence of ERP systems on information technology, remarkably little has been written on the history of ERP. Conceptually, ERP is a combined set of modules that share a database and user interface, and which supports multiple functions used by different business units. Because the ERP modules share a single database, employees in different divisions—for example, accounting and sales—can rely on the same information for their specific needs without any time lag. A major selling point of ERP systems was not that they provided particularly good functionality in any operational area. In actuality, they provided very basic functionality in all areas, but, because the applications shared the same database, anything that occurred in operations was immediately reflected on the accounting side. It was an argument tailor-made for executives who would never have to personally deal with the functionality limitations of ERP systems. Gartner is credited with naming ERP systems. The term ERP (Enterprise Resource Planning) was adopted from the term "material requirements planning" (MRP) or "manufacturing requirements planning" by simply removing the "M" and replacing it with an "E." This was done because, while ERP systems contained the MRP supply and production planning method, they also contained sales, financial accounting, and materials management functionality. Companies found that planning was only the beginning of ERP's limitations. ERP is now well known for many limitations in its ability to present analytical data to customers. The shortcomings of ERP in this regard are a strong precursor to the growth of the separate business intelligence market, a market that was not supposed to have developed if all reporting was done within the ERP system as had been originally projected by proponents of ERP. My research into ERP continually reinforced a central concept that ERP rarely impresses the companies where it is installed. Instead, ERP tends to be discussed as a rite of passage.

CHAPTER 3

Logical Fallacies and the Logics Used to Sell ERP

Many of the arguments that are habitually made in favor of ERP are, in fact, nothing more than logical fallacies, and because of this it is important to review briefly the definition of "logical fallacies."

Proponents of ERP use a number of logical fallacies in the quotations used throughout this book, and when they occur, I will be referring to these proponents by their official names. In fact, it is quite surprising **how many** of the quotations from ERP proponents fall into one or more categories of logical fallacy, and realizing this led me to read a book specifically on logical fallacies in order to make sure I was able to identify all of them properly. When a topic leads one to actually read a book on the topic of dishonest argumentation, this is a good indicator that something is wrong with the information that is being researched. As always, in the absence of actual evidence, it becomes quite easy to fall into the use of logical fallacies.

Logical fallacies are arguments that use poor reasoning. They fall into the following categories:

1. *Presumption:* Failing to prove conclusion by assuming the conclusion in the proof.

2. *Weak Inference:* Failing to provide sufficient evidence.

3. *Distraction:* Providing conclusion with irrelevant evidence.

4. *Ambiguity:* Failing to provide the conclusion due to vagueness in words, phrases or grammar.[18]

The Logical Fallacies

In this book, at least **one** of the following logical fallacies is presented in the form of a quotation from ERP proponents. These logical fallacies are listed below:

1. *Appeal to Probability:* Takes something for granted because it might be the case.

2. *Appeal to Fear:* An appeal to emotion where an argument is made by increasing fear. The fear discussed may have a kernel of truth, but the proposer actively increases this fear in an attempt to win the argument and gain influence over decision-making.

3. *The False Dichotomy/The False Dilemma:* Forces a choice between two alternatives, when there are, in fact, more than two alternatives. One alternative is the proposer's desired course of action and one alternative would have an unacceptable outcome.

4. *Argument from Ignorance:* Assuming a claim is true because it has not been proven false.

5. *Argument from Repetitions:* States that, as it has been discussed, it is not worthwhile discussing.

6. *Shifting the Burden of Proof:* Does not prove a claim, but asks for the claim to be disproved.

---

[18] Wikipedia

7. *Argument to Moderation:* Assuming that the compromise between two positions is always correct.

8. *Argumentum ad Hominem:* Evading the standard requirement to provide counterevidence through the use of a personal attack.

9. *Hasty Generalization:* Leaping to a conclusion on the basis of a small sample of data.

10. *Argumentum ad Numerum or Argumentum ad Populum:* Appeals to a widespread belief; the fact that many people believe it, means it must be true.

11. *Appeal to Authority:* Where an assertion is deemed true because of the position or authority of the person asserting it.

12. *Appeal to Accomplishment:* Assertion is considered true or false based upon the accomplishment level of the proposer.

13. *Appeal to Consequences:* Where the conclusion is supported by a premise that asserts positive or negative consequences from some course of action in an attempt to distract from the initial discussion.

14. *Wishful Thinking:* An appeal to emotion where a decision is made based upon what is pleasing to think to be true.

15. *Argumentum ad Novitatem/Appeal to Novelty:* Where a proposal is claimed to be true/superior because it is new or modern.

The Logic Used to Sell ERP

The following chapter will cover the logics used to sell ERP systems. Each will be analyzed. However, a brief explanation of each will help set the stage.

1. *Y2K (Year 2000):* This was the concern related to the ability to properly calculate dates in software that had been developed back when there was a very small amount of data storage available and developers saved storage by just using the last two digits of years.

2. *Single System:* Companies have preferred to have a fewer number of systems. Developers and consultants know that developing specific purpose applications provides better usability, functionality and maintainability

than applications that try to cover a broad range of areas. However, this reality is unappealing to those that purchase software.

3. *Best Practices:* Best practices are essentially a single best way of doing something. Best practices can be applied in software or outside of software. However, in software the concept of best practices is that software vendors can review how many companies do something and choose the best way to incorporate it into their functionality.

4. *Integration Benefits:* Hypothetically, if either a single system or a very few number of systems can be purchased and used by a company, it will reduce the integration costs.

5. *One Size Fits All:* Under this logic, if the purchasing company simply agrees to use the software the way the ERP software vendor recommends, often following the logic of best practices, that all or nearly all companies can use the same ERP software.

6. *All Industries:* This logic is that ERP systems, and particularly ERP systems from the larger vendors because of their experience in so many industries translates into the software vendor being able to build the functionality in their software to be implemented in any industry and to meet most of their requirements.

7. *Cost Reduction:* Related to—or build upon the previous logics—that since all of the previous logics are true that this will result in a reduction in costs. Also based upon the idea that if a company concentrates its software purchases from fewer vendors that costs will decline.

8. *The Logic of ERP Driven Improved Financial Performance:* This was the logic that ERP would be a pathway to improving the financial performance of a company. At one level, the financial performance was predicted to come from the improved operations of the company—but a second proposal was that the purchasing of an ERP system would signal to other entities, which the purchasing company desired to impress that the purchasing company was making a serious effort to improve. These entities could

range from customers, suppliers, potential acquiring companies as well as Wall Street.[19]

In order to keep make the book as understandable as possible, these logics have been divided into three chapters. Chapter 4 covers best practices, Chapter 5 covers integration, while Chapter 6 covers all the *other* logics listed above. We will begin with the logic of best practices.

---

[19] In interviewing people for this book, this logic was proposed not only by those with a financial bias, but by those who worked in best of breed vendors and had nothing to do with perpetuating ERP software or consulting sales. On several occasions the proposal was made in stark terms that the actual business or operational value of the ERP system was not all that material, and that the ERP purchase was valued for its ability to signal to partners and observers that the company was "serious." There is little doubt that many ERP systems were purchased, in part, to signal success to other entities—however, the hypothesis to be tested is "did this actually work." That is where the purchasing companies the recipients of a halo effect due to the purchase that lead to better financial performance. (For instance due to suppliers providing them with more stock or better terms, to customers buying more from them, or to Wall Street being more positively predisposed to recommending the company.) This question is addressed in Chapter 7: "The High TCO and Low ROI of ERP."

CHAPTER 4

The Best Practice Logic for ERP

Best practices are a frequent topic of conversation for ERP software vendors, in other types of enterprise software, and in consulting. Most likely the concept of "best practices" stemmed from a kernel of truth that some practices deemed more efficient or more intelligently designed could be adopted from some companies and placed into software. However, the idea rapidly became overused and turned into a virtual addiction for the marketing departments of vendors and consulting companies.

According to ERP "best practices," only those business processes deemed a best practice by an ERP vendor have value and all processes should conform to these best practices, an idea sometimes referred to as "genericizing" a business. This viewpoint places the ERP software vendor in the position of determining what is and what is not a best practice. Sure enough, 100 percent of the time, the best practice **is contained** in the functionality that the ERP software vendor has developed.

There are some interesting questions that should be asked whenever any software vendor makes a statement about best practices:

1. Who decided something is a best practice?[20]

2. Was the best practice put to a vote?

3. Was it deemed to be so by an expert?

4. If item three is affirmative, where is the research to support the notion that a way of doing something is a best practice?

What a person who asks these types of inflammatory questions (yes, simply asking for evidence is considered inflammatory with regard to best practices) will find is that in the vast majority of cases, the practice is a "best practice" simply because the proposer declares it to be so. There is no research and no explanation as to how it was determined to be a best practice. Furthermore, if two different ERP systems—both of which are based upon best practices—diverge in some way on how to do things, which one is actually performing the best practice?

Best practices sound suspiciously like something that one is asked to take on faith—and they are. Eugene Bardach, a professor of public policy, analyzed claims of best practices in his field and found that best practices **are not based upon research**.

> *"Appearances can be very deceiving. On closer inspection, it often turns out that the supposedly 'good' practice is not solving the problem at all. Inadequate measurement plus someone's rose-colored glasses were simply producing the illusion of mitigating the problem. It may also turn out that, even if good effects have truly occurred, the allegedly 'good' practice had little or nothing to do with producing them."*

The further one gets from actual implementation, and the less experience one has with working with software, the more likely one is to believe that software can encapsulate best practices. Because the term "best practices" is so general, it does

---

[20] I have also noticed that the less a person knows about the application, the more willing they are to use the phraseology of best practices. Among experienced implementers, best practices are considered nothing more than marketing hyperbole.

not invite debate and is designed to be accepted without criticism by the audience. It is a bit like someone pledging allegiance to goodness: what could possibly be wrong with goodness? However, even experts will disagree as to what is a best practice in their particular field. Also, who decides what constitutes "best"? For example, when a company asks me how to set up software to meet an intended objective, there can be several alternatives. Let's take a look at two common issues that are faced with configuring software.

1. One way might be simpler, process more quickly, and therefore update more frequently, and is easier for users to understand and maintain.

2. Another way might be more complex; process more slowly and thus update less frequently, and is quite difficult to troubleshoot.

In this example, which method for achieving the same objective is the best practice? If there is only one best way of doing something, why does software provide so many alternatives for doing the same thing? A specific example can assist you in understanding how unhelpful the concept of best practices is in making decisions from among competing alternatives.

The Car Versus Truck Best Practice Example

Let's take the example of two automobiles: one sedan and one truck. I currently own a Honda Accord, but have been thinking of buying a four-wheel drive Toyota Tundra. These are two very different automobiles built for different purposes. Both score very well in reliability, which I consider a best practice; that is, I prefer high quality cars that require infrequent repairs. However, could the fact that they both use an internal combustion engine and pneumatic tires be considered best practices? These are two of the most important inventions in human history, so I suppose I would not object to calling them best practices. But on the other hand, every car I look at offers the same thing, so while they are best practices, *they are not differentiators*. Am I interested in comparing best practices that are not differentiators? I would say probably not. The Toyota has four wheel drive, which can be a best practice if you intend to take the car off road, but is an unnecessary and extravagant option if one does not intend to use the vehicle in this manner. Four wheel drive decreases gas mileage after all, and the knobby tires required to go off-road, ride roughly on a paved road.

So should I sell my Honda and buy the Toyota? Well, there are a number of factors, such as how much I will be using the vehicle for commuting versus taking my jet ski to the lake and going camping. The vehicle's benefits to me change depending upon the situation. There are some best practices, such as reliability, that are important to me, but may be less important to other people. For instance, neither of these are particularly stylish. However, the Land Rover is very stylish and has the best practice of four-wheel drive. If anyone has ever sat inside of a Land Rover with a leather interior, I think we can agree that their interiors are a best practice (that is, they feel very nice). However, in order to get the stylish ride, one has to pay a great deal more, and give up the Japanese reliability for English reliability. So how do I decide on my vehicle with all these competing best practices?

I hope I have shown that there is a reason that people don't take the concept of best practices to buying an automobile, or really to any other purchasing decision, and this is because the concept is ridiculous. People look for a series of trade offs in characteristics until they find a desirable compromise, and then make their purchase decision. It does not happen now, and will not happen in the future, that your friend will announce that he based his new car purchasing decision on best practices.

I used the example of cars because most everyone has at some point made a decision to purchase a car and because cars are relatively easy to understand. However, the concept of best practices is equally unhelpful and even problematic in making distinctions between things that we do not know as well. As my expertise is supply chain software, I know that making supply chain software decisions based upon best practices does not make any sense. This is elementary for me, because I have spent more than a decade and a half analyzing and configuring supply chain software and work with it almost every day. However, because I don't know much about accounting software, if someone were to propose that accounting software can be purchased based upon best practices, it would seem to me to be a tenable statement, but only because I do not have the content expertise to truly analyze the claim. Certainly there are things that are desirable in accounting software that could be deemed "best practices." For instance, it is desirable that the program post the actual quantities entered into the database, rather than using a random number generator. It is desirable that the program not crash and delete the last five hundred accounting entries. However, once we get past the rather banal areas of functionality, there will be considerable debate as to what are best practices.

The fact that the concept of best practices was such an effective marketing ploy is yet another indicator that many of the executives that analyzed ERP software sales pitches did not have sufficient experience with the software they were purchasing to know that software couldn't be purchased using best practices as a measure.

Now that I have covered best practices generally, I will provide specific examples of how best practices have been used to sell ERP, and what the results were. To some degree, all the ERP companies used best practices to sell their software. I happen to focus on how SAP uses the term because I have spent so much time over the years reading their literature.

SAP Best Practices and SAP's Marketing Machine

SAP uses a number of marketing and sales concepts repeatedly to gain and maintain clients in the marketplace. "Best practice" is one of these concepts. Now, there is nothing wrong with marketing and sales concepts that are accurate, but SAP's best practice claims are inaccurate. It's important to understand that SAP marketing messages work not only to get SAP clients, but also to **control how their client interprets their software during implementation and after a go-live**. SAP claims that their software is built around best practices: because they are so large, they can say they have "standardized" their software around the best practice. They use this concept on their accounts in multiple ways:

1. To initially sell the software.

2. To control the implementation process so that the client is guided into doing things "the SAP way."

3. To shut down dissension on the part of users who often don't like the applications or how they have been configured.

4. To prevent executives from analyzing the underlying reasons of why users are unhappy with the implementation (i.e., dissatisfaction is the fault of users, never the application; this can be summed up with the statement, *"look we are fantastic, your users just don't get it!"*).

How SAP Uses the Concept of Best Practices to Control the Implementation

SAP lists best practices in several areas on its website. I have included the following screenshot of best practices from this web page.

SAP BEST PRACTICES
SIMPLIFY. STREAMLINE. SAVE.
Executive Summary

SAP BEST PRACTICES FOR CHEMICALS V1.603 (U.S.)

SAP Best Practices - 36 years of experience with over 40,000 customers, collected in a library of SAP packages. Designed with industry experts, tried and tested preconfigured modules cover up to 80% of an industry's requirements.

SAP Best Practices quickly turns your SAP software into a live system, personalized to meet your needs.

- Use SAP Best Practices to reduce costs. Customers who use SAP Best Practices have been able to reduce their consulting and customer project resources by an average of 50%.
- Use SAP Best Practices to save time. Project time is reduced by an average of 22%.
- Use SAP Best Practices to reduce risk. Preconfigurations and step-by-step documentation help to avoid mistakes.

The SAP Best Practices building block library provides additional flexible configuration options. For example, you can combine this version with a cross-industry package, such as SAP Best Practices for CRM, to cover all of your business needs.

Here, SAP claims that because they are so big, all best practices are included in their software. Secondly, they propose that customers who use best practices have been able to reduce consulting costs by 50 percent and reduce mistakes. But, wait one second; aren't best practices simply inherent within SAP? **Does one have to choose between a best practice implementation and a non-best practice implementation**? What constitutes a best practice implementation? This is all extremely confusing, as well as logically inconsistent.

SAP's Confusion on the Topic of Best Practices

It brings up the question "what exactly are best practices in SAP?" Here is another quotation on the topic of best practices.

> *"SAP Best Practices Based Upon Netweaver—SAP Best Practices*
> *provide a toolset that helps IT and functional project team members*
> *to quickly deploy functionality in SAP solutions—from SAP*

NetWeaver, to core SAP applications. The toolset comprises a mix of step-by-step instructions, preconfiguration, sample master data, code samples (where applicable) and end-user training—organized by technical or business scenarios that you might want to implement in your landscape. Below you will find the SAP Best Practice versions that support the implementation of SAP NetWeaver components."
— SAP

In this quotation, SAP classifies best practices as a **toolset** or accelerator made up of instructions, pre-configuration and sample master data. But let's back up a few steps here and take just one example. What do best practices have to do with the master data samples? Best practices are supposed to be business process functionality that is in the system naturally. Master data should be kept up to date and validated with the business, which I suppose could be said to be a best practice; this is not something you can bake into the application unless you mean to make the software transparent and easy to use. In that case you are enabling a best practice; **you are not modeling a best practice yourself**.

Overall, SAP's best practice seems more like a jumpstart toolkit that contains a combination of things that are best practices. The paragraph goes on to say that there is a NetWeaver component to best practices. How can this be? NetWeaver is **comprised** of the infrastructure components of SAP, so what do these have to do with business process functionality best practices?[21] I suppose one could say that their infrastructure follows best practices, with the business, software, toolkits and infrastructure software all based upon best practices.

SAP hammers away at this theme throughout their documentation, but because they apply it to everything they do, it begins to sound like unsupported conjecture— and that is the best-case scenario. The worst-case scenario is that SAP employs marketers who can't keep their story straight and have limited English and logic foundations. Also one questions how serious SAP is about their NetWeaver best practices because, when I reviewed this material, all of their links to supporting content on the web page were broken.

---

[21] NetWeaver also encompasses their business intelligence application, at least according to their literature, but no one refers to this application as part of NetWeaver; it is simply marketing hyperbole.

The answer to these questions? SAP just does not know; they are confused themselves as to how to use the term "best practices." SAP simply smears the term, like cream cheese on a bagel, on almost everything they do. With SAP, simply calling standard SAP documentation a "best practice" will somehow (magically) allow projects to go live much more quickly. In this case a best practice is an incantation. It's difficult to take a vendor seriously when they are so undisciplined as to the use of their terminology.

SAP finishes off the proposal by declaring that best practices enable SAP implementations to go live in 4.2 months. This is not true; in all my years working with SAP I have never seen any SAP module go live in 4.2 months. This is another problem with credibility: SAP implementations are measured in years—not months—and anyone who works in SAP knows this. So where is this number coming from, and what module is SAP talking about? Where is the evidence for this? No evidence is ever presented.

The Negative Effect of Best Practice Claims on Projects

If only best practice claims ended when the software was sold, that would be one thing; however, the conversations regarding best practices pass from sales to the consultants who are supposed to make good on these claims during the implementation. When you repeatedly tell a customer that they will get best practices in every dimension if they buy your software, unfortunately they don't forget this. As with any promise that can't be fulfilled, SAP consultants are put in a difficult position. I would know—I have been one of these consultants.

On many of my projects, the term "best practice" becomes a punch line. The individuals in the implementing company come to realize that there is no such thing as best practices. Jokes such as, *"But wait…it's okay because it has best practices,"* or, *"All we need on this project is just more best practices!"* are quite common. Because the marketing and salespeople don't actually work on projects or with software, they do not know this. After realizing that they had been bamboozled by SAP Sales (accompanied by a healthy dose of cynicism about best practices), I heard senior members of my client declare, *"We don't want to hear anything more about best practices."* In the implementation phase, best practices lose all credibility.

Non-ERP Uses of the Term "Best Practices"

SAP is certainly not the only company that uses the term "best practices" as a marketing construct for the purposes of business development. Consultants from large consulting firms also like to use the term, and use it in a way that is almost always misleading. I once worked with a consultant who created a custom adjustment for a safety stock problem in a way that was completely inadvisable: I would consider it to be a worst practice. He then proposed that weekly delivery frequency was best practice. He essentially suggested that any technique that he wanted to employ was a best practice. On this project, I learned that twice-a-week delivery was a best practice; who knew that how frequently a product is delivered could be a best practice? It isn't.

Consulting companies are constantly using the term "best practices" to sell work. However, as with best practice claims made by ERP vendors, no evidence exists that what the consultants promote as a best practice is, in fact, that and this is because they have no evidence; it's an opinion. It's one thing to say that this or that is one's opinion from experience. But it's something else to gusset up this opinion as a best practice—with zero evidence—simply because one would like to have their opinion carry more weight. It is also common to hear from the client that the consulting company did not seem to offer best practices once they were on the project. The reason is simple enough: once one gets into the details of the actual recommendation, they look a whole lot less like "best practices" than they did from a distance.

Criticizing Pre-existing Systems

Best practices have been very useful to ERP vendors as a way of giving them permission to criticize a potential customer's pre-existing systems. Sales and marketing is about changing perceptions to encourage a purchasing decision. One way of doing this is to increase the purported virtues of the item to be purchased (in this case, the ERP system). Another way is to lower the perceived value of the customer's current item. Using the term "legacy" to describe all previous systems, and the term "best practices" to describe ERP systems, is highly effective and an impressive feat of rhetoric because it ignores the important fact that the legacy system had been customized for the business requirements, while the ERP system had not. Essentially ERP vendors appealed to a central concept: how things are done in other organizations must be better than how things are done in the potential customer's company. This is a reversal of the *"not invented here,"* philosophy which proposes, "anything *not invented here."* This is explained in the following quotation:

> *"'Don't assume newer is necessarily better,' advised Project Manager Ellen Harmon of the Washington State Community and Technical Colleges Center for Information Services. Harmon considers her existing legacy system to be just another, older ERP. 'We actually have an ERP that has been developed over the last 18 to 20 years for specific clients, and because of that, this ERP is very focused on these particular client needs.' The case is the same at other universities. 'Their legacy systems have been developed to meet their specific needs and are tailored to their environment,' said Harmon. 'An ERP vendor might say your system is old, and therefore is bad, and we will sell you this new system. But it is a legacy system, too.'"* — Promise of ERP System

This quotation brings up an interesting question: what is the definition of "legacy"? An ERP vendor may be selling a system that has an older code base than the "legacy" system it is replacing. Interestingly, the designs of many of the ERP applications sold today are extremely dated, and yet they are never referred to as "legacy." To a software salesman, other people's systems are legacy, but your systems are never legacy. One might ask why this is the case. The reason is not hard to determine. "Legacy" is a term of propaganda[22] that is applied to systems

---

[22] A term of propaganda is a term that is designed to influence but is only hypocritically or inconsistently applied. If a state labels violent actions perpetuated against its interests as "terrorism," but conversely labels its own violent actions against others as supporting some virtuous end (which it defines and appraises in terms of meeting that end) then terrorism becomes a term of propaganda—which is, in fact, its most common usage. Whether a term becomes identifiably a term of propaganda is not related to the term itself—which can have any authentic derivation, but from the context of the term's repeated usage. By this measure, the term "legacy" is a clear term of propaganda because while ERP vendors routinely accuse customers they would like to sell software to as having legacy systems (often combined with the term old, so old-legacy) no ERP vendor has ever admitted to having any legacy software.

Terms of propaganda are extremely effective at short-circuiting critical thought and resistance to ideas, by speaking in a type of code, which implies certain judgments, but without providing evidence. In fact the entire purpose of the use of terms of propaganda is to influence without evidence.

that the designator would prefer to denigrate as a pretext for proposing another system.[23] If you work in ERP Sales, then all pre-existing systems in the companies to which you would like to sell your ERP software are legacy. The ERP system you are selling—no matter how dated—is never referred to as legacy. Therefore the term "legacy" has two meanings: the actual definition ("an old method, technology, computer system or application program") and the real meaning—any system that you would like to replace. However, many decision makers missed an important detail of infrastructure technology management, as explained in the following quotation:

> *"IT analysts estimate that the cost to replace business logic is about five times that of reuse, and that's not counting the risks involved in wholesale replacement. Ideally, businesses would never have to rewrite most core business logic; debits must equal credits—they always have, and they always will. New software may increase the risk of system failures and security breaches."* — Wikipedia

Many companies relearned this fact about computer systems. Many of the cost overruns of ERP systems were related to replacing business logic.

Conclusion

Best practices have been a deep well that ERP vendors have repeatedly drawn from in order to support multiple objectives. ERP vendors do not attempt to hire professional researchers to validate their claims regarding best practices because a) most of what they are proposing is simply how their software works—and is not a best practice, and b) customers generally don't question the best practice claims made by ERP vendors. Generally all that is needed to convince companies that a software vendor has best practices is if the software vendor has marketing documentation that declares the existence of best practices, and if that software vendor is generally successful selling its software and has significant brand recognition.

---

[23] *"As opposed to impartially providing information, propaganda, in its most basic sense, presents information primarily to influence an audience. Propaganda often presents facts selectively (thus possibly lying by omission) to encourage a particular synthesis, or uses loaded messages to produce an emotional rather than rational response to the information presented. The desired result is a change of the attitude toward the subject in the target audience to further a political, religious or commercial agenda. Propaganda can be used as a form of ideological or commercial warfare."* — Wikipedia

CHAPTER 5

The Integration Benefits Logic for ERP

Enhanced integration was one of the major selling points of ERP. The hours of PowerPoint presentations that have been created since the first ERP systems were sold describe the great cost savings and integrative benefits that implementing companies would receive from a "solution" where all the main applications used the same database. One of the assumptions about purchasing an ERP system was that the buying company would implement all of the modules and decommission their current software. I discussed this briefly in a previous section. This oversimplified assumption was self-serving for the concept's promoters, but not considerate of the buyer's needs. The fact is, some of the company's pre-existing applications could not be replaced by ERP, and for a variety of very good reasons. Here are several of the common scenarios in which companies that implemented ERP found themselves:

1. In rare cases, companies eventually replaced every one of their existing systems with ERP, representing a perfect match with what the ERP salespeople proposed.
    a. Some companies that followed this approach paid far more than they had anticipated customizing the ERP application to replicate part of their current solutions.

   b. Some companies that followed this approach lost functionality and wished they had not gone 100 percent ERP, but could not go back once they had completed the switch.

   c. In some cases they removed all existing systems and replaced them with ERP, and were happy with both the cost and the functionality that resulted from doing this.

2. In most cases companies **did not implement all of the modules that they had purchased.** General estimates are that an average of 60 percent of the modules were implemented and 40 percent were unimplemented. Other times, companies implemented all the modules but were unable to decommission pre-existing applications because those applications did something of value for the company and it would have required too much work to customize their new ERP system. This topic is covered separately in the section on "One Size Fits All Versus Customization."

Contrary to most assumptions, ERP systems provide no advantages in terms of integration to other systems, and in fact present several disadvantages:

1. *No Integration Advantage:* ERP systems were not designed to integrate well with any other system, with the exception of electronic data interchange (EDI). ERP vendors proposed that their systems integrated better with the other applications that they offered for sale. However, this contention is also of a dubious nature. Many applications sold by ERP vendors (Oracle being a good example) resulted from acquisitions. These applications have different heritages than the vendor's ERP system. Oracle created adapters for these disparate applications, but their value is questionable.

2. *Low Quality and Uncompetitive Middleware:* Even when the non-ERP vendor applications were developed internally (such as with SAP), the applications did not integrate very well. I have many years of experience integrating external planning systems to SAP, and contrary to what ERP vendors say, not as many of these applications integrate to the ERP system as what is led to believe. Part of the reason for this is that ERP vendors are not necessarily **good at creating middleware** (the software that connects other software). In fact some (such as SAP) are not at all skilled in creating integration applications of any type; they seriously lag behind the best

vendors in the middleware software category.[24] Therefore, the **customer ends up purchasing middleware by default from a company that is uncompetitive in that software category.** I discuss this in the following articles that I wrote to inform companies that they were greatly underestimating the short-term and long-term effort involved to maintain the SAP ERP to SAP APO integration application called the "core interface" (CIF). The CIF is an SAP-to-SAP interface, but while it can be brought up quickly, is so maintenance-intensive that over the long term, I debate whether it is better to develop an adapter from scratch.

http://www.scmfocus.com/sapplanning/2011/05/19/why-i-no-longer-recommend-using-the-cif/

http://www.scmfocus.com/sapplanning/2012/10/30/the-cif-administrator/

The Unfortunate History of ERP "Integration"

Here is a much more effective solution than I have described above: ERP vendors should never have been allowed to procure other vendors. They should not have created external applications, and instead should have published an integration standard and allowed the middleware vendors (those that were actually skilled at creating middleware) to create the adapters.

ERP companies had no interest in this solution. Instead they intended to use their position at their customers to sell in more software. Often this software was poorly integrated and uncompetitive with best-of-breed applications (outside of just the ERP system). In this way, the ERP companies put their own interests ahead of their customers' interests, as explained in the quotation below.

> *"Of course, as soon as companies began buying these products, it became clear that enterprise software was another chunk—a much larger and better integrated chunk to be sure, but still a chunk—of software in a complex architecture of IT systems that desperately needed to talk to one another and exchange information. The vendors*

---

[24] Actually, there is no reason to assume that ERP companies would be good at middleware as it is a completely different type of software from ERP software.

created clunky, proprietary methods of connecting their systems with others that have improved over the years, but that misses the point. The architecture of these systems, in a broad sense, was just like the ones that they were intended to save you from monolithic, highly integrated and difficult to change.

"The high degree of integration envisioned in the R&D lab was tenuous at best inside most customers." — CIO

ERP systems integrated some areas of functionality used by the company, but certainly not all things. And again, because most companies have so many applications, there is still a lot of integration work that needs to be done. A 2001 study **found that ERP increased the need for integration**.

"ERP technology does not offer an integrated solution but amplifies the need for integration." — ERP and Application Integration

*"Although ERP is touted as a single architecture, ERP applications usually contain different generations and sources of technology. Third-party applications are acquired and amalgamated into the platform, sometimes by name only. In total, this makes the environment complex for the customer and difficult to change over time. ERP suppliers have become **system integrators.** [emphasis added] The sheer size and number of applications makes moving all the applications forward a difficult task. Application functionality often lags."* — ERP Alternatives

In terms of ERP's impact on application integration, companies did not see any immediate benefit. But was there a longer-term benefit? Unfortunately after extensive searching I was unable to find research data that compared what portion of the IT budget was consumed by application integration before and after ERP implementations. The shortage of research on this topic is particularly galling when one considers how confidently those **who sold ERP systems predicted that integration costs would decline**. However, findings in the study *ERP and Application Integration* are not promising.

> *"ERP technology does not offer an integrated solution but it amplifies the need for integration. Enterprises faced integration problems when they attempted to incorporate other applications with an ERP system. Only EDI applications were integrated successfully (81 percent) with ERP infrastructure. This high integration rate derives from the fact that EDI technology follows similar concepts to AI (application integration).* — ERP and Application Integration

This shocking quotation states that ERP *"amplifies the need for integration."* Because ERP applications are self-integrated, the problems that ERP systems have with interfacing with other systems is actually higher than the benefits derived from ERP's self-integration. That is yet another amazing statement.[25] The quotation goes on to say as much.

> *"All observations discussed above indicate that ERP systems cannot be seen as a reliable solution to integration problems as ERP modules co-exist with other applications. Additionally, there is a need to integrate the ERP solutions with other applications. However, this incorporation causes serious problems, especially with companies."* — ERP and Application Integration

ERP may have been a step forward for the integration of the ERP modules (as I describe in "Case Study #4 of ERP Misuse: Intercompany Transfer"), ***but they were a major step backward for all other forms of integration***. However, the only important measurement is **total** integration—not how much the integration effort was reduced for **one** application. It is important to consider that no study **demonstrates that ERP systems reduce integration costs, and at least one study demonstrates that ERP increases integration costs**. This exact statement may be used the next time you hear a person promote the integration benefits of ERP systems: ask him/her to produce the study that demonstrates this "well-known fact."

---

[25] Although considering the difficulties I have witnessed with ERP system integration with Tier 1 ERP vendors first hand, I probably should not be surprised.

My personal experience with SAP ERP is that it is an extremely difficult system to write interfaces for, but this level of difficulty varies for each ERP vendor. SAP does not even export data in rows and columns but instead uses something called an intermediate document or IDOC. This is a hierarchical document, which is difficult to read, and time consuming to write transformation scripts for which will convert the document into rows and columns. Unfortunately IDOCs also change between versions of SAP, and a single movement of a character by one place can render the integration unusable and require a script rewrite. However, when these IDOCs will be changes is not communicated by SAP—so you find out when something breaks.

Generally, others who work in SAP ERP integration tend to agree that SAP is difficult to integrate to, although they will not go on record as saying so; if one wants to continue to work in an area, it's better, of course, to keep silent. I did not perform an analysis of all ERP systems to determine integration difficulty. I found it far easier to integrate to some of the lighter open-source ERP systems, but it is no coincidence that these applications were developed more recently than Tier 1 ERP applications. Although there are too few studies upon which to base any definitive conclusion, it is equally possible that ERP systems increased the integration costs that were incurred by companies. But either way (whether it is a wash, or whether ERP increases integration costs), the story does not have a positive outcome. That they most likely did not reduce their integration costs (and quite possibly increased their integration costs) would be quite surprising to companies that gave up so much for the promise of an integrated system.[26]

ERP and the Internet

There are few people (with the natural exception of ERP vendors themselves) who will debate the notion that ERP systems are walled off from the Internet. Since ERP developed, the Internet has become an important force, and web front-ends have greatly improved application interfaces and the ability to connect various applications. This point is reinforced by a 2007 article in the *MIT Sloan Management Review*.

---

[26] Companies made the error of defining "system" too narrowly. One must look at the overall integration costs, not simply whether one large system, like ERP, is self-integrated.

"Just as companies were undertaking multiyear ERP implementations, the Internet was evolving into a major force, changing the way companies transacted business with their customers, suppliers and partners."

Here's a concrete example of how far integration has come since ERP first became popular. I recently installed an application called Yesware off of the Internet. Yesware automatically integrates with my Gmail to track emails, and also integrates with a variety of CRM applications; this is integration across Internet servers by different companies that have decided to cooperate. These are two applications that are communicating over the Internet to one another—each performing a different function—and each aware of what the other is doing. All of these adapters are created for me, and all of them work transparently. My integration effort was limited to clicking a button to install Yesware, and rebooting my email client. This is clearly the future of application integration across the Internet. Of course, none of this capability existed when the concept of ERP was developed. In stark contrast, most ERP software—and particularly on-premises ERP software—still sits with dated application interfaces and manually intensive ways of interacting with other systems. Getting most ERP systems to do what I did with Yesware, Gmail and a CRM application would be a major initiative at a company and cost quite a lot of money. This point is brought up in the following quotation:

> *"As the web increasingly becomes the medium for information exchange, your on-premises ERP is increasingly a disconnected silo from the rest of the world."* — Craig Sullivan, NetSuite

Rootstock, which covers much of the functionality of an ERP system, does in fact work in a similar way, as it is part of the Salesforce.com platform. But Rootstock is more of an exception, most ERP systems do not work this way.

Errors in the Platitudes Regarding ERP Integration

Executive decision-makers, and also researchers, have some general misunderstandings about the state of integration. The following is an example.

> *"Information integration is a key benefit of ES. This integration can replace functionally oriented and often poorly connected legacy*

software, resulting in savings in infrastructure support costs. Furthermore, improvements in operational integration enabled by ES can affect the entire organization and therefore can positively impact firm performance. As discussed below, ERP systems also provide benefits in the area of transaction automation, SCM systems provide more sophisticated planning capabilities, and CRM systems facilitate customer relationship management." — The Impact of Enterprise Systems on Corporate Performance

This and other similar quotes confuse **functionality with the system that brings that functionality,** in much the same manner as those who confuse an economic system with a particular form of production. For instance, one who says that industrial capitalism is good because *"people bake bread for profit"* misses the fact that bread has been baked and sold for thousands of years before the existence of industrial capitalism. Such logic intends to prove that the desired output—the bread in this case—is best accomplished within an industrial capital system versus some alternative system. Let's parse this quotation in order to analyze it properly because there are a number of assumptions contained within:

1. *New software can replace poorly connected legacy software:* It's unclear why the legacy systems were so poorly connected in the first place, as was suggested by ERP salesmen during the early stages of ERP's popularity. All enterprise software faces these integration challenges. Notice the researchers in this quote are using "ES" not "ERP," as they propose that all enterprise software has advantages in integration over legacy systems. However, no evidence is given as to why this is true. Systems must be made to work with other systems. An ERP system is more integrated to itself, but as I have explained earlier, that **is not the end** of the story. Furthermore, enterprise software infrastructure costs **have not declined** due to ERP being implemented. Some vendors do allow their applications to be integrated easily to other systems that are not their own. However, SAP and Oracle do not promote ease of integration to systems from other vendors. Instead they sell closed systems to companies, getting them to buy into the SAP or Oracle ecology. Even if one vendor provides multiple systems, the systems will not share the same database, and many of the adapters that are offered are of questionable value.

2. *ERP systems also provide benefits in the area of transaction automation:* This may have been a differentiator when ERP was first introduced, but now less expensive applications like RootStock or ERPNext can automate transactions as well as any Tier 1 or 2 ERP system.[27] There is no reason to give up so much leverage and pay such a high price for automation that can be found in applications from software vendors that are far easier to deal with.

> *"ERP systems replace complex and sometimes manual interfaces between different systems with standardized, cross-functional transaction automation."* — The Impact of Enterprise Systems on Corporate Performance

This paper was written in 2005, but manual interfaces between systems were replaced a long time ago. There is standardized cross-functional transaction automation, but that is only within the ERP application and not between the ERP application and the many different systems with which it must interact.

> *"Another benefit of ERP systems is that all enterprise data is collected once during the initial transaction, stored centrally, and updated in real time. This ensures that all levels of planning are based on the same data and that the resulting plans realistically reflect the prevailing operating conditions of the firm. For example, a single, centrally developed forecast ensures that operational processes remain synchronized and allows the firm to provide consistent order information to customers (Bancroft et al. [1998])."* — The Impact of Enterprise Systems on Corporate Performance

Unless the company uses an ERP system only (and no other systems), the example above is inaccurate. On projects I have spent quite a lot of time working on how the supply chain planning system will pull data from the ERP system and on how the planning recommendations will be sent back. Data pulls from the ERP system for reporting or business intelligence must also be timed, and this is not

---

[27] Both of these applications will be showcased in Chapter 11: "Alternatives to ERP or Adjusting the Current ERP System."

a real-time feed. These are just two examples, but all systems that are connected to ERP face the same questions and limitations. The only thing that is true about the above quotation is that the ERP system has updated transactions (stock transfers, purchase orders, financial transactions), but this functionality is generic.

The *Over Integration* of ERP Systems

The much-promoted internal ERP integration is **described universally as a virtue** and as a system with no corresponding downside. I do not exaggerate when I say that I could not find anything published about the disadvantages of ERP being self-integrated. However, systems that are so integrated limit a company's flexibility to meet its requirements, although at first it can be difficult to see how this is the case. When a system external to the ERP system makes a decision, that decision/output must be converted so that the receiving system can understand and use the transaction. A transaction can have multiple dimensions (a payment processed between two locations/entities, a shipment sent between two entities, etc.). The problem is that ERP systems offer a limited number of options per dimension (as with most systems; however with ERP systems there is a catch), and when the company has a requirement that cannot be met by a transaction that exists in the ERP system, customization must be performed. Customization rarely works smoothly and becomes something that the company must maintain in the long term. Customization of ERP systems is one of the most expensive customizations a company will ever pay for, as it means hiring programmers at the top of the market and developing from within the ERP software vendor's environment. This is explained in the following quotation.

> *"'We could have written ABAP code, but the cost of ABAP programming and maintenance is enormous,' says Bill Waters, MMS's director of information services. With Oberon, MMS saved the initial programming effort and will save even more whenever it upgrades its packaged apps. Oberon provides prebuilt connectors between the two systems and is committed to maintaining and enhancing these links so MMS doesn't have to."*

ERP applications are not known as efficient applications to customize.

"The problem is the lack of a full set of application development tools in ERP packages. Major ERP vendors may publish APIs, include a low-level programming language, reveal their underlying data schema, and even provide some customization tools. But they don't usually provide testing and debugging—or much of the other functionality developers expect." — ERP: More than an Application

Customization is a near universal requirement for ERP systems. According to IDC, 87 percent of respondents to their survey performed moderate to extensive customizations in their ERP system, and estimates from other sources move that figure up to 96 percent.[28, 29]

"During the past two years, Data Exchange has invested several million dollars in its systems overhaul. A good portion of that money went toward custom coding. 'Each business is unique,' Malchicoff says. 'We did a gap analysis of what Oracle could do and what we needed to do for our business.' The company wrote nineteen modules comprising fifty thousand lines of code for such things as logistics, process control, and data mining. That effort was just as significant as deploying the ERP software—and it cost just as much, an amount Malchicoff had to calculate as part of his ROI analysis." — Making ERP Add Up

More than a third of small to mid-sized manufacturers that use on-premises ERP operate between two and three releases behind the most up-to-date version of their ERP system.[30] Furthermore, because the modules within the ERP system are so tightly integrated, there is no easy way around the module in order to connect directly into the ERP's financial system. The reason for this is clear: if we use ERP's inventory system as an example, the inventory system must have the full information on all inventory movements, even if there is no standard way for the ERP's inventory module to process the movement.

---

[28] From *Maintaining ERP Systems: The Cost of Change*, Michael Fauscette, IDC, 2013.

[29] On the other hand, Mint Jutras (an independent research-based consulting firm), estimated that 96 percent of companies required moderate to extensive customization.

[30] *ERP as a Living System: The Power of Community-Driven Product Enhancement.* Plex.

While many articles describe ERP systems as inflexible, they miss out on the distinction that I just explained: part of this inflexibility is due to the over-integration of ERP systems. In one article that followed the "ERP is inflexible theme," the IT analyst firm IDC did an excellent job of elaborating on one aspect of ERP inflexibility:

> *"ERP systems in general are not designed to be flexible; in fact, most are designed to provide and automate repeatable business processes. While there is substantial benefit to this automation and predictability, there are also risks and costs."*

"Inflexibility" is used as an umbrella term for many ERP shortcomings, but "over integration" is the term *I use to explain the specific problem that results in inflexibility*. ERP systems cannot represent all the different business processes that exist in a system, and its introverted design limits a company's ability to implement these business processes without considerable and expensive customization.[31] In fact, one of the reasons that ERP vendors and consulting companies make so much mention of best practices **is because ERP's coverage of business processes is restricted, making it necessary for ERP vendors to have a readymade argument to use to convince the company not to implement its preferred—and in many cases valuable—business process, and to accept a substitute that requires the company to make all the adjustments.**

How ERP Sets the Integration Agenda for All Other Applications

If you check out the websites of non-ERP vendors, you will find them littered with various certified (by the ERP vendor) integration adapters. (Most of these certified adapters are more marketing sizzle than reality as the link below describes.)

http://www.scmfocus.com/sapintegration/2011/11/15/what-are-saps-vendor-integration-certifications-worth-on-projects/

---

[31] These customizations are the "gift that keeps giving." They mean long-term maintenance costs as explained by this quotation.

"In general, each customization needs to be rewritten or readdressed each time there is an upgrade, so the value of an organization's ERP support largely depends on whether or not it is able to improve or upgrade the software without worrying too much about the effects on its customized components."— Third Party ERP Support: When it Makes Sense

It is crucial for non-ERP vendors to show their ability to integrate with the applications of ERP vendors. During the presale presentation to the customer, they often pay homage to the customer's existing ERP system (particularly to SAP and Oracle because of their popularity in the market) by talking about the great relationship they have with that ERP vendor, and if possible, by discussing the details of as many joint implementations as possible. I have been critical of software vendors in the inventory optimization space who dilute their own message by stating in their marketing literature that they "work with" ERP vendor functionality, rather than replace ERP functionality. These vendors have sophisticated solutions with functionality that is head and shoulders above what can be found in ERP systems. Yet, because they are concerned about offending the ERP vendor, they are as non-confrontational as possible, even to the point of misrepresenting what their applications actually do. For instance, when they refer to SAP on their websites, they could not be more deferential, as I explain in the following article.

http://www.scmfocus.com/enterprisesoftwarepolicy/2011/11/16/everyone-in-enterprise-software-is-afraid-of-the-big-sap-bully/

This is the power that many ERP systems have. Other vendors are fearful of contesting the ERP system directly or showing how their systems are superior. That is, the other vendors self-censor. These are not the workings of a transparent market; the power and veto authority of the ERP software vendors influence the information provided by other vendors that do not even sell ERP software.

CHAPTER 6

Analyzing the Logic Used to Sell ERP

In this chapter we will analyze all of the other logics used to sell ERP systems. Each one of these logics was important, but somewhat easier to explain than best practices and integration. That is why these shorter explanations were assigned to a single chapter.

Y2K (Year 2000)

Many ERP purchasing decisions were made because companies simply felt they needed to have ERP. This interpretation was often based either upon fear (such as the Y2K fear that drove so many ERP implementations) or a herd mentality. ERP presented itself as a silver bullet for the Y2K issue: instead of adjusting the dates on all of a company's old systems to ensure they would work properly post year 2000, they could be replaced—swept away by a shiny new ERP system. Fear of Y2K was a main component of the ERP vendors' sales strategy.[32]

> *"Slater (1999) discusses the breadth of such problems as*
> *he notes that 'companies buy multimillion-dollar software*
> *packages only to find out they don't work—or at least they*

---

[32] The appeal to fear is another logical fallacy.

don't work well—for one of their key business processes.' The reason, Slater suggests, is that ERP software is so hot, the flames fanned by consultants and the technical press cause companies to simply push forward without dealing with such key restrictions." — Technology Monoculture[33]

One System to Rule Them All: The Single System Logic for ERP

A primary logic used to promote ERP purchases was that the ERP system would be the only system that an enterprise needed to purchase, as explained in the following quotation.

> *"The name is now Enterprise Resource Planning (ERP) systems to suggest that all information systems required for the management of a manufacturing enterprise are part of the solution."* — Process Industry ERP Requirements

When companies that purchased ERP found that ERP did not meet all their business needs, the next idea put forward was to implement the ERP software first, and then to connect non-ERP software (the so-called best-of-breed software) second. This approach is considered desirable because ERP is known as the backbone or the "mother ship," with the other applications connected to it.

The initial idea behind ERP systems was that it would amalgamate many applications into a single system, thus reducing application integration issues. This concept is encapsulated in the quotation below:

> *"Many technical reasons exist including the replacement of disparate systems into a single integrated system."* — Hitt, et al., 2002

This turned out never to be the case for the vast majority of companies that implemented ERP software.

---

[33] *"The Year 2000 problem (also known as the Y2K problem, the Millennium bug, the Y2K bug, or simply Y2K) was a problem for both digital (computer-related) and non-digital documentation and data storage situations which resulted from the practice of abbreviating a four-digit year to two digits."* — Wikipedia

"The majority of respondents reported that an ERP system fulfills only 30 to 50 percent of IT requirements. As a result, many companies did not abandon their legacy systems but they tend to integrate the functionality from disparate applications." — ERP and Application Integration: Exploratory Survey

"Most pharmaceutical companies have invested in enterprise resource planning systems (ERPs), but few get enough bang for the millions of bucks these platforms cost. It's as if they bought a Lexus loaded with all the extras, but only use it to drive around the neighborhood. 'Most [drug] companies are using ERP for the bare minimum,' says Eric Bloom, vice president of information technology at Endo Pharmaceuticals. To realize the promise of ERPs, pharmaceutical manufacturers must fully integrate them with plant systems such as manufacturing execution systems (MES), quality management systems (QMS), and software for targeted applications such as radio frequency identification, or RFID. For most pharmaceutical companies, the biggest issue is, 'How deep should I take my ERP system into manufacturing?' says Roddy Martin, vice president for life sciences industry strategies at AMR Research in Boston." — Realizing ERP's Untapped Potential

And this is the constant problem: ERP does very little for manufacturing. This is true; in fact most ERP systems were never really designed with much manufacturing functionality.[34] Often ERP is discussed in terms of its MRP/DRP functionality, but even this is quite basic, not only from a sophistication level, but also from a usability perspective.[35] They can perform basic functions on the inventory level—such as goods issue and goods receipt—but ERP systems cannot be considered as much more than a starter kit for any manufacturing company. Many companies have tried to "get more out of their ERP systems" by pushing them in directions where they were never designed to go (of course, with a healthy dose of

---

[34] One of the few exceptions to this is the ERP system Process Pro. This is an ERP system that is focused on process industry manufacturing. It profiled in the SCM Focus Press book, *Process Industry Manufacturing Software: ERP, Planning, Recipe, MES & Process Control.*

[35] This topic is covered in detail, as well as all of the methods available for both supply and production planning in the SCM Focus Press book, *Supply Planning with MRP/DRP and APS Software.*

customization), but companies that rely on ERP systems in this way cannot hope to properly leverage the available manufacturing software, and will always run their plants at a much lower level of efficiency than companies that adopt the more sophisticated and nuanced IT strategy that is laid out in the book, *Replacing ERP: Breaking the Big ERP Habit with Flexible Applications at a Fraction of the Cost.*

ERP systems never replaced all of the legacy systems in companies that purchased ERP. Therefore, this prediction was spectacularly incorrect. Secondly, ERP vendors did not stick with this principle (of ERP being the only system a company needed to purchase) for very long, as the next section will describe. The fact that they moved away from this logic so quickly makes one wonder if they ever actually believed it themselves.

The Changing Story on ERP's Ability to Meet All Requirements

Soon after the major ERP vendors had saturated the market for ERP software, they began to develop specialized applications for things like supply chain planning, business intelligence, customer relationship management, etc. That is, when the opportunity presented itself, they immediately contradicted their own logic that **they had used to convince so many companies to buy ERP systems**. Curiously, a review of the IT/business literature at the time shows that the business/technology press did not seem to pick up on the fact that this new strategy was completely inconsistent with the earlier arguments used to convince companies to buy ERP. I could find no articles that explained how inconsistent the new diversified application strategy was with ERP vendors' own statements made previously.

ERP vendors moved away from providing only ERP systems for several good reasons.

1. *The Single System Approach Was Unworkable:* The single system concept was never anything more than marketing hyperbole—and only a credible hypothesis for the naive, and it is unlikely the vendors actually believed what they were selling. There was simply no way that an ERP system, with its elementary approach to all functionality, could meet all the needs within companies.

2. *Sales Growth:* Once ERP vendors had sold their ERP applications into most of the large and medium to large customers globally, they needed to develop more applications in order to increase their sales. In some cases they could have simply added functionality to ERP; however, this strategy would **not have maximized the ERP vendors' revenues, as they would only get upgrade revenues from their existing clients.** The *trick* was to sell new applications to their existing clients, without having the clients remember that a main justification for purchasing ERP in the first place was that it would cover all of a company's requirements with a single application that contained all of the best practices (more on that later in this chapter). The ERP vendors relied upon both their consulting partners as well as the compliant IT analysts (the ERP vendors being the largest sell-side revenue stream of the major IT analysts) to never point out this minor detail to customers.

Account Control

From the competitive positioning perspective, selling an ERP system to a company was ***one of the best ways ever developed to sell more software (after IBM unbundled software from hardware in 1969)*** into the same company in the future and to control the account. Rather than looking out for the interests of the buyer, account control is how third parties—such as software vendors and consulting companies—manipulate (or direct, depending upon your preference) their customers into following the desires of the third party. IBM was the first vendor to perfect account control and many of their strategies (including how they leased their machines, the prices they charged, the way they dealt with their customers, etc.) was based upon account control strategies. Account control is behind how major consulting companies interact with their clients. For instance, large consulting companies want more of their own consultants on a project rather than the consultants from the software vendors, because they receive more billing hours and because it helps them control the account and control the information that their customers receive. At large software purchasing companies in particular, the enterprise software market cannot really be understood without understanding account control.

Once the software vendors had implemented the ERP system at a company, their relationship with that company was based on the fact that they were responsible for that company's largest IT purchase. They had the network effect on their side. The misinformation they passed to their clients reinforced the dubious concept that ERP was somehow the keystone application. They pushed the "boogie man" of integration: that is, while the integration from other applications they sold would naturally integrate to their ERP system, the software from other vendors was an "unknown," a guarantee that other software from that vendor would integrate to the ERP system at a reasonable cost or in a reasonable timeframe. That was the story anyway; a future section in this chapter will explain why this was never true.[36]

This integration argument is particularly compelling because the ERP system is considered the central application for a company—the application to which other applications must integrate. This granted ERP software vendors the same type of monopoly power over their customers that Microsoft gained through controlling the operating system on PCs (but in the case of Microsoft, their applications actually did work better than competing applications on Windows, although they often made sure of this by postponing information about Windows from becoming public until the new version of Windows was released—they could have very easily released the APIs earlier). This monopoly allowed ERP vendors to unfairly compete: they told clients that their applications had a head start on integrating to the company's ERP system. In the example of SAP and Oracle, the integration benefits were far more illusory. I can recall my shock when I analyzed the prebuilt adapter that extracted information from SAP ERP b SAP BI/BW. It was clear that Development had done the absolute minimum required in order to mislead potential customers into thinking that they could pull a large variety of data from SAP ERP into BI/BW. Instead, what customers really received was a starter kit. Companies like SAP and Oracle promptly took full advantage of this market power, and this enabled them to charge top dollar for all of their

---

[36] This is repeated by SAP consultants whose opinion seems eerily similar no matter which you speak with. Their opinion is that they would *"prefer to stay"* away from using non SAP applications—because "they have seen integration issues on previous projects." Actually, this is not a fact-based opinion—it is an example of financial bias. SAP consultants maximize their income when they simply mirror the viewpoints of SAP itself. This bias is the same as that demonstrated by consulting companies—the "best" software solution for their "clients" is the solution they can make the most money from. If one can predict the advice based upon which selection maximizes the income of the advisor, it is not an objective opinion.

applications, and furthermore to easily compete with applications that were far superior to their own applications.

Overall, this power was abused in so many ways that it would be tedious for my readers if I listed them all. But I will mention one of the more creative ways, which was developed by SAP: their pseudo partnership program with other vendors promised entry into SAP's enormous client database,[37] when in fact the program was an intelligence-gathering operation by SAP to allow it to steal intellectual property from their "partner" vendors, thus helping them to backward engineer the application (this was called the xApps program, which I describe in the article below). As far as I can see, SCM Focus was the only media entity to call this program what it was.

http://www.scmfocus.com/inventoryoptimizationmultiechelon/2010/01/its-time-for-the-sap-xapps-program-to-die/

http://www.scmfocus.com/enterprisesoftwarepolicy/2012/01/27/how-common-is-it-for-sap-to-take-intellectual-property-from-partners/[38]

Once again the IT/business press and IT analysts failed to explain what this program actually was, and in fact they lauded it. And once again they were proven incorrect when the program died and did not lead to a new golden age of integrated applications (no surprise, it was never intended to).

The upshot of all of this was that the ERP vendors were in an excellent position to sell more software into these accounts. These new non-ERP applications all have their own platforms, and while they have adapters or interfaces to one another, they are each a separate application; they each have a different database and sit

---

[37] Which happened very rarely.

[38] As is the norm, the Federal Trade Commission (the government entity responsible for enforcing anti-trust legislation) does nothing in the enterprise software space but rubber-stamp its approval of acquisitions. There is little incentive for the FTC to enforce anti-trust laws that most of the US population does not know exist, and when members of the FTC are actually looking for jobs in the companies that they supposedly regulate. Like the SEC, the FTC is an excellent place to network and obtain well-paying jobs in the industry.

on different hardware. In fact, many of these new applications are acquisitions: after a software vendor acquires another software vendor, they typically develop a marketing program to inform all current and potential customers as to how well the new applications will work together. ERP clients who purchased applications that Oracle had acquired were actually worse off than if the software had been **left independent and adapters had been written to Oracle ERP.** The long-term history of software acquisition clearly demonstrates that as the price of software goes up, development of the application stalls, and in many cases the application is simply subsumed into what is often an inferior application. There are a number of cases where the acquired application is mostly eliminated. But the acquiring company also acquires the customers and is able to increase their prices now that they have removed a competitor from the marketplace. Software acquisitions have only two winners:

1. *The Acquiring Company:* They eliminate a competitor.

2. *The Senior Members of the Acquired Firm:* They receive a handsome buy-out as compensation.

Despite promises on the part of the acquiring vendor, often the reality for integration does not change much after an acquisition. For example, many of these software vendors already had adapters that connected to Oracle ERP. However, the acquisitions allowed Oracle to increase the price of the acquired application because they became part of the "Oracle Suite."

As a result, companies that implemented ERP are essentially back where they started before the move to ERP, except now they rely more on external application development through commercial software rather than internal application development. While buying companies were sold on the idea that ERP would take a "blank sheet of paper" approach, to the present day companies *still* have complex landscapes with many applications that have separate databases and separate hardware and are **interfaced,** but not **integrated—just like before the whole ERP trend began.** Promises of a single integrated system simply never came about.

One Size Fits All

One of the original arguments used to sell ERP systems was that the standard functionality of the ERP system could be used *"right out of the box."* But as ERP systems are customized so regularly, this sales pitch has long since been forgotten. Not only was this assumption wrong, it was fabulously wrong. According to research by Mint Jutras, around **96 percent of respondents to a survey** stated that they did moderate to extensive customization to their ERP systems. This has been my experience on projects as well, but I can say with confidence that most companies that purchased ERP systems had no idea they would eventually customize their ERP systems to the degree that they did.

I once had a defense contractor as a client. They discussed their interest in replacing a system that connected to the Department of Defense. At first it seemed as if we could take the logic for the system and port it to SAP ERP. However, the more we analyzed the application, the more it became apparent that this application was so specialized and had taken so much time and effort to build that the best course of action was simply to keep the system but integrate it to SAP ERP.

It looks much easier to decommission software when you do not personally use it and are not aware of everything that it does.[39] Over the decades, many companies have gone through this identical process. Very little is written on the subject of system replacement errors, which led IT decision-makers to greatly underestimate the degree to which companies faced this issue of being unable to decommission systems that were performing important tasks, and to **overestimate how well the ERP implementations at other companies were faring**. Companies bought ERP, often without knowing how specialized their own applications were, and they ended up having to integrate many more systems to the ERP system than they had expected, as well as to customize their ERP systems more than

---

[39] The proposal that all these customized applications could be replaced by generic ERP systems was ludicrous, but was accepted by decision makers precisely because they lacked familiarity with their own systems.

they ever anticipated. As a result, their ERP systems consumed a much higher percentage of their IT budgets than forecasted.

All of the above happened, but to a much larger degree, on the Air Force's Expeditionary Combat Support System (ECSS) initiative, a now notorious program to take all of the Air Force's support systems (two hundred and forty legacy systems) and move them to Oracle ERP. Some salespeople at Oracle, with the help of Computer Sciences Corporation (CSC), essentially convinced the Air Force that they could replace almost all of the supply chain and accounting systems maintained by the Air Force with their ERP system. One billion dollars later, the Air Force finally concluded that their project objective was not possible; further extraordinary customization would have been required, which have taken another **one billion dollars to complete. Therefore the Air Force cancelled ECSS.** The functionality to replicate the Air Force's existing systems did not exist in Oracle ERP; CSC and Oracle would have been required to both generalize the Air Force's processes and rebuild an enormous quantity of custom functionality in Oracle. Oracle and CSC took one billion dollars of taxpayer money and did not deliver an operational system.[40]

If there ever was a project doomed before it even began, it was the ECSS project. The Air Force bought the *"we can cover all your requirements"* argument pitched by ERP salespeople and consulting companies in the most extreme way. Think about this: Oracle ERP can cover two hundred and forty systems encompassing decades of specialized development? That is quite a proposal. But to various degrees, most other companies have fallen for the same argument. This inability to use "out of the box" ERP functionality is a theme that is often repeated, as explained in the quotation below:

> *"... many mid-sized companies quickly find that different business units have slightly different requirements, even for commodity processes like accounts payable and human resources. These local differences may arise from regulatory and compliance considerations, or simply a resistance to changing current working practices because of the organizational impact. Faced with inherent limitations and no viable way*

---

[40] Air Force Considering Alternatives to Key ERP.

to overcome them, the team responsible for expanding a legacy ERP implementation is often forced to create multiple ERP instances (each with its own database), resulting in:

- *Dramatically increased cost, complexity and effort for corporate reporting and analytics*
- *Added complexity to support transactions among business units*
- *Increased hardware and IT administration cost and complexity*
- *A natural tendency toward local optimization at the expense of overall visibility and effectiveness"*—Is Your ERP Creating a Legacy of Frustration?

Planning for the Inevitable Customization

Unanticipated customization greatly increases implementation costs and durations. It also means long-term and largely unanticipated maintenance as the customized ERP systems face issues caused by each new version (or at least major version) of the ERP software released by the vendor. The customization required for ERP systems has demonstrated that these systems are **simply starter kits** rather than completely usable systems. Companies went to tremendous expense to do nothing more than replicate functionality that was, in many cases, working perfectly well and meeting requirements in the legacy applications that ERP salespeople criticized as archaic. The reality is that the ERP salespeople had no idea what they were talking about. Most had never worked in the field of software implementation and, like trained parrots, were simply repeating catch phrases. It is the height of arrogance to state that you "know" that the functionality in your software is better than the functionality residing in a customer's system, when you have never seen nor analyzed their system and probably would not understand it if you did.

ERP's Operational Improvement

One of the logical arguments used to sell ERP was that it would improve the company's operations. I was able to find several studies that showed a correlation between operational improvements in a company and ERP implementations. A quotation from one of these studies, *Which Came First, IT or Productivity,* says the following about operational versus financial performance.

> *"Our results demonstrate that ERP adoption strongly influences operational performance (inventory turnover, asset utilization, collection efficiency) and labor productivity but has a negligible impact on measures of financial return or profitability."*

This is a bit of a paradox. Shouldn't improvements in operational efficiency be evidenced by improvements in financial performance? The study *ERP Investment, Business Impact and Productivity Measures* says the following about productivity, and brings up some interesting issues in terms of when the productivity is measured.

> *"Given that most of our data is before and during implementation, this suggests that higher performing firms tend to adopt ERP and that their performance is at least maintained and possibly improved by ERP adoption. Our data does not have many (data) points post implementation.*

> *"Our results on performance analyses using the same specifications previously, consistently show that firms have higher performance during the implementation than before or after.*

> *"It also suggests that the paybacks begin to appear before the projects are completed—probably the most reasonable interpretation is that many of the components of an ERP adoption are completed and operational before the firm declares the project to be complete."*

In all likelihood, this statement is not true. Companies declare their systems "live" as soon as they can, and rarely does it happen that the systems are operational but not declared "live." More commonly the system is declared live before the implementation is complete. Much fine-tuning is required post "go-live" to get the applications working as required. Frequently I am part of a team that tunes live projects.

> *"Alternatively, it could be that many of the 'belt-tightening' organizational changes such as changes in inventory policy or*

*reduction in the number of suppliers begin to generate gains fairly
quickly, even if the more technical aspects of the project have not yet
been completed."*

Other alternative explanations for the productivity gain during the implementation could be the "Hawthorne Effect." The Hawthorne Effect is when subjects in a study improve their performance because they **know** they are being observed. The researchers do not mention this as a possible reason for the post go-live performance improvement, but it is a quite obvious and likely explanation.

> *"There is a productivity gain during the implementation period,
> followed by a partial loss thereafter. When value added is used as the
> dependent variable, the gains are 3.6 percent during implementation
> with a loss of 4.7 percent for a net gain of –1.1 percent (t= .8, not
> significant)."*

I list the Hawthorne Effect as a likely reason for the gain during the implementation because the software is not yet operational; therefore, the benefit cannot be from the software itself. Regardless of the reason, the short-term gain in productivity—followed by an overall loss of productivity—is not a happy ending or a compelling reason to purchase an ERP system. When the actual benefits of ERP are evaluated (evaluated from any dimension one cares to choose), the fact that ERP is seen as a "mandatory infrastructure"—as stated in many articles and as is generally accepted in companies—does not seem to compute.

The "All Industries" Logic of ERP

ERP vendors have been adamant that their software can be used for any industry. SAP has many different industry solutions. However, when one examines these advertised capabilities, the actual functionality is often lacking. These SAP industry solutions are ***really more marketing constructs than usable functionality,*** and because the marketing is so good, it took me years of working on SAP projects to figure this out. While I have not worked with every industry solution, I have worked with many of them, and none of them have been as advertised. Most of the time the ERP system is implemented without using the functionality of the "industry solution." SAP industry solutions are designed to get executives in purchasing companies to think that SAP can meet the unique requirements within **their** industry, but in truth, SAP tends to offer generic functionality as a base, which they sell to most of their customers. Then they add some functionality for the specific industry, which is of dubious implementation value, but serves as the "hook" to make the executive decision-makers think the software has been customized for their needs.

I have worked on several SAP implementations for repetitive manufacturing. Repetitive manufacturing is a manufacturing environment where the production is continuous and the equipment investments are high, as is the rate of production. Late in one project, it finally came out that the repetitive manufacturing functionality was not worth turning on. As a result the implementing company decided to forgo the functionality and stick with the standard discrete functionality with a few adjustments. SAP got the sale by pitching repetitive functionality down to the eleventh hour. But the company wasted an enormous amount of time discussing whether or not repetitive manufacturing functionality would be used. As a very experienced SAP consultant (from SAP itself) once stated to me, *"There is really more sizzle than steak to SAP repetitive manufacturing."*

This issue of "there not being much there" is repeated throughout SAP industry solutions. Among prospects there seems to be some confusion on this topic. Just because a software vendor has a number of customers in a particular industry does not mean that their software serves that market or provides the necessary functionality. But with applications from name-brand vendors, so much of the purchasing decision is based upon the brand yet so much of the ERP system is customized by many clients. Across all industries, one of the greatest unheralded "helpers" is probably Excel. It might be more accurate to say in airport advertisements "XYZ ERP vendor + Excel is used by four out of five top chemical companies." An honest statement—but obviously not as catchy. Simply put, many executives buy software to advance their careers, because other companies buy it, or because the marketing and the salesmanship dazzled them.

As discussed in the next section, another common division between manufacturing companies, who are the most common implementers of ERP systems, is the division between discrete and process industry manufacturers.

The Example of Discrete Versus Process Manufacturing Requirements
In discrete manufacturing (e.g., automobiles, toys and tools), usually there are multiple input items and a single output item. However, in process manufacturing, where the final item cannot be broken down and converted back to the original input products (i.e., cheese cannot be disassembled into its original components, but an automobile can), one input item can convert to multiple output items, or multiple input items can convert to multiple output items. All of these relationships can be easily modeled in a spreadsheet.

The finished product of process manufacturing is not simply the **assembly of the input products**, but is in fact an altogether transformed item. For example:

1. One cannot unthread fabric to get to the original spools and restock the thread as inventory.

2. Once crude oil is cracked into jet fuel, kerosene, tar, etc., it cannot be reconstituted back into crude oil.

3. In some types of process industry manufacturing, the input product is literally "gone." For instance, when coal is converted into electrical energy, it cannot be converted back into coal.

So what common and important capabilities are typical of process industry manufacturing? The software vendor TGI, which states the following capabilities within its Enterprise 21 software application, can demonstrate the requirements for process manufacturing planning.

1. *"Supports infinite-level formulas with yielding at the top level or ingredient level and rank-ordered ingredient substitutes*

2. *Products can have global formulas or unique facility-specific formulas*

3. *Supports scalable batches*

4. *Supports recipes through the integration of formulas and associated processing instructions and notes for use during batch process production*

5. *System maintained version and revision control with a fully integrated engineering change order process*

6. *Formulas support nested formulas and intermediates and can have infinite notes and instructions*

7. *Supports online review of formulas via single-level and multi-level explosion*

8. *Multi-level where-used functionality enables rapid access and mass change to all finished goods using specific ingredients, intermediates, and nested formulas*

9. *Formulas and recipes are easily duplicated and updated for the same product or a new product*

10. *Formulas are pulled into work orders or batches for tracking and recording of actual ingredients consumed or backflushed at defined standards"*[41]

Batch functionality in SAP can be enabled, which is used for batch process manufacturing. Batch functionality is a very popular requirement for all types of batch manufacturing (including manufacturing such items as bakery items, paint, glass, specialty chemical, and pharmaceuticals, as is explained in the SCM Focus Press book *Process Industry Manufacturing Software: ERP, Planning, Recipe, MES & Process Control*). Batch functionality allows specific batches (e.g., a batch of pharmaceuticals from a single production run) to be tracked. Batch manufacturing can be enabled in SAP ERP as described in the following link:

http://help.sap.com/saphelp_SCM700_ehp01/helpdata/en/48/aae32a8740356 ce10000000a421937/frameset.htm

However, batch functionality is well known as a major headache to enable. Batch management was added as an afterthought, even though it is foundational to a batch management ERP system and also a process industry ERP system. SAP ERP was designed to work with discrete manufacturing, which simply has quite different requirements. This is not just an issue with SAP ERP, but of ERP generally, and not just with ERP as a software category, but with all manufacturing enterprise software sold to process industry customers. This is a topic in the SCM Focus Press book, *Process Industry Manufacturing Software: ERP, Planning, Recipe, MES & Process Control*.

---

[41] http://www.scmfocus.com/sapplanning/2012/06/28/backflushing-sap/.

The following quotations talk about how enterprise software designed for discrete manufacturing customers is sold to process manufacturing companies.

> *"For IT chiefs like Pam Haney, IT director at Irvine Scientific, a $28 million life sciences company, issues of competitive advantage are overshadowed by ever-present customization needs with her ERP system. 'What we're faced with is having to deal with ERP packages that are not designed for process manufacturers.'"* — Why ERP Systems are More Important Than Ever, CIO

> *"Originally business information systems for manufacturing companies were designed for discrete manufacturers, not process industries. These systems targeted industries such as automotive, consumer electronics, machine tools, etc. The discrete manufacturing sector produces piece parts to form subassemblies, which are then combined to form the final product. Nearly all ERP suppliers have built their information systems to support the business functions of discrete manufacturers."* — Process Industry ERP Requirements

Very specific requirements exist in process industry manufacturing companies that must be met one way or another.

> *"Today, process manufacturers have a proliferation of products. These products are produced using the same equipment or using existing processes downstream but at the same site. Because of the number of products now flowing through the same cost center, using financially-based cost systems to develop accurate, individual product costs is difficult, sometimes impossible. Furthermore, as multiple methods evolve for producing the same end item (whether in a sister plant or with newer technologies in an existing plant), the setting of standard costs must reflect a weighted average cost. This type of costing can only be done using an ERP system designed for the process environment."* — Process Industry ERP Requirements

Businesses require solutions that have been designed from the ground up to meet their requirements, not software that attempts to meet their requirements. ERP vendors claim they can address the specific requirements of manufacturers by appealing (successfully) to all industries with slick marketing literature, yet with the barest level of functionality. Right now, thousands of companies have made unplanned customizations to their ERP systems because ERP vendors told them that the software would cover their industry-specific requirements when, in fact, they could not. So much money has flowed into Tier 1 ERP vendors who have provided generic solutions and left promises regarding industry-specific functionality unfulfilled, that money has been prevented from flowing to solutions that could have been developed to offer companies software that meets their requirements. This is another example of a prediction make by many ERP vendors that helped them get sales, but has been bad for their "customers" and bad for the enterprise software market overall.

The Single Instance Logic of ERP

Another main selling point of ERP was that a company would be able to move to a single instance of their ERP system. This idea continues to be a selling point of vendors such as SAP, even though **in most cases only smaller companies actually have single instances of ERP.**

> *"An 'instance' refers to the number of discreet versions of ERP software you have in your company. The original vision of ERP was that companies should have a single instance—that is, a single implementation of the software running on a single database— that serves the entire company. It would mean no duplication of information in different departments or in different geographic divisions and thus better integration and information quality across the company. Upgrading the software would also be easier than with multiple customized instances of ERP across the company." — The ABCs of ERP*

Historically companies have been unable to move to a single instance of ERP, yet no one questions why, especially since this is presented as such a desirable end state. As the complexity of a company increases with the addition of regions or subsidiaries, the value of having a single instance of an ERP system, with only one database, becomes questionable. Vendors certainly know this, but present a single instance as a desirable option with benefits to the customer anyhow.

The reasons why companies are unable to move to a single ERP instance are well documented and are not going away; some of the major causes are listed below:

1. *Database Management and Query Efficiency:* ERP systems are supposed to be single database systems, which belies their integration. There are issues with reduced efficiencies at higher data volumes, but what is the value of having sales figures from different subsidiaries that may have no relationship to each other in the same sales order table? For instance, if a user performs a query for all sales in a quarter, do they mean the sales of subsidiary one or subsidiary two? How do proponents of the single instance ERP system consider the increased complexity of the data in their presentation of this solution?

2. *Which Region/Division/Subsidiary Gets Its Way?:* If different regions do business differently, and they must move to a single instance, which region gets the system configured or customized to its requirements? What happens to the productivity of the company that gets its configuration adjusted for no other reason than the desire to normalize the functionality across the subsidiaries so that the move to a single ERP system can be facilitated? Most often it is the region with the political power (i.e., the region where the headquarters are located), and has absolutely nothing to do with logic or what is best for the business. I have been on several global implementations and I would recommend to any independent contractor who could choose between a global implementation and a regional implementation to choose the latter. Global implementations are exercises in one region enforcing its will upon the other regions. At one client site, the region with the headquarters simply left out functionality that was available in the application when the new application was explained to the other regions. The functionality they left out would have allowed the application to be configured differently. They did this to prevent the other region from choosing a configuration

that was different from what they had already decided upon. The region that selected the configuration assumed that the configuration was right for everyone seeing as **they** had selected it. They called this the "Global Template," which was a convenient way of getting the other regions to do things their way.

3. *Negotiation Leverage:* A single ERP system is viewed as a cost savings because more business is aggregated to one vendor. Surely this is a one-sided view on the matter: single sourcing also increases the negotiating leverage of the vendor (why they like it so much). What happens when the ERP vendor knows they have 100 percent of a customer's ERP business? Well, this is just the starting point for Tier 1 ERP vendors; their eventual goal is to replace all enterprise software used by the company with their other applications, to turn the client's IT infrastructure into a monoculture, and to staff the IT departments with 100 percent compliant executive decision-makers. If this sounds vaguely familiar, it is because it is the same desire of every major IT consulting company. When I first got into consulting, my partner at KPMG explained to me that our role was to "penetrate" the client and then "radiate" through them.

4. *What About Functionality?:* Looking from 30,000 feet up, it's easy to state, *"If we use one system we can save money."* However, there is another side of the equation: the value that the system provides. When a company moves to a monoculture, having regions/divisions/subsidiaries—the people who actually know the business, reduces the functionality benefits—choose their own solutions. This leads to the next point.

5. *How Much Does Customization Increase With a Single Solution?:* Proponents of a single instance ERP leave this point out of the analysis, and for good reason. Using a single instance ERP system will mean more customization or, as so many IT proponents prefer, taking a wrecking ball to the business requirements. However, customization translates to real money, both up front and in long-term maintenance, and the costs must be estimated as part of a strategy of moving to a single instance ERP.

6. *What About Flexibility?:* Moving toward a single ERP system has negative implications for the flexibility of the company. If the acquisition is eventually sold, what is the cost of breaking the acquisition out from the combined ERP system?

Hold on to your hats! Tier 1 ERP vendors are not doing this analysis—or have done the analysis but don't want their customers to know the truth. Instead they continue to **bang the gong** of single instance ERP. In truth, that a single ERP system was never a realistic proposition should have been apparent to buyers from the very beginning. It is now well documented that the vast majority of companies **do not** have a single ERP system, and the reasons are quite well explained. The following quote is just one of many examples.

> *"Well, it sounded great on paper, but unfortunately reality bites. The stories started to leak out—multi-million dollar never-ending ERP projects, high profile ERP project failures, inability to tailor the deployment to local subsidiary needs, and over-tapped local IT resources overwhelmed by a monolithic on-premise ERP deployment. And if a division is run as a profit-center, these kinds of deployments can quickly paint red all over the P&L."* — The Decline of Single Instance ERP

Multiple ERP systems in companies are now the norm, and not just two or three ERP systems as the quotations below explain.

> *"On average, big companies worldwide are running five SAP instances, while almost four in ten have more than six, according to a study from IT services firm HCL Technologies."* — When SAP Sprawl is Cool, ZDNet

> *"The concept of a single monolithic system failed for many companies. Different divisions or facilities often made independent purchases,*

and other systems were inherited through mergers and acquisitions.
Thus, many companies ended up having several instances of the same
ERP systems or a variety of different ERP systems altogether, further
complicating their IT landscape. In the end, ERP systems became just
another subset of the legacy systems they were supposed to replace."
— The Trouble with Enterprise Software

According to one IDC survey, 72 percent of respondents were running more than one ERP system. People will say that multiple ERP instances can be consolidated into one, but in most cases that is simply not practical. There are a number of very good reasons as to why a company cannot reasonably be expected to move to a single ERP instance.

> *"'A lot of people run multiple instances because of geographic reasons,*
> *regulations, or business-sector reasons,' Illsley said.*
>
> *"If you've got part of your business that is outsourced, for example,*
> *you'd probably want to run an instance that your outsourcing provider*
> *could use and that would be different to the one you would want to*
> *keep inside, so that it's easier to do things like that."* — When SAP
> Sprawl is Cool, ZDNet

So, while some companies have moved to a single instance of ERP, most have not and will not in the future. It is easier for smaller companies to move to a single instance, and more difficult for larger companies, particularly companies with subsidiaries. We are now three decades into the ERP phenomena and only a small portion of single instance ERP systems are in use. So why is it still considered a realistic goal to move to a single instance of ERP? Apparently many Tier 1 ERP software vendors think it is quite reasonable. However many companies are turning a deaf ear to this message and are, in fact, now far more frequently exploring the concept of a two-tiered ERP system.[42]

Two-tiered ERP

Two-tiered ERP systems are a trend in ERP, but there is little research on the impacts of two-tiered ERP strategies and how they differ from what companies are doing anyway with multiple ERP systems. Once again, the marketing is far ahead of the evidence. Remember that a previous concept—service-oriented architecture (SOA), which has now flamed out with respect to ERP systems—was also supposed to be a "savior" for ERP. I work on projects where ERP is omnipresent, yet after so many SOA books published and so many ERP vendor marketing documents written, SOA has yet to show its face on any of my projects.[43] Major ERP vendors made a lot of noise about supporting SOA, but SOA never fit their business model because it reduces their account control; there was no reason for

---

[42] In fact, "a single instance" is not only frequently fool's gold in ERP, but in other software categories as well. For instance in supply chain planning, one of the worst things that a consultant can do is get staffed on a global "single instance" project. This is because it leads to seemingly endless debates with the other region as to how the system will be configured and each region believes that the configuration settings that work for them should be the ones to be used. Typically, the region where the company is headquartered gets its way—and the other regions must deal with a system that is poorly configured for their needs. On one project, the region that first implemented the software deliberately mislead the other regions as to what functionality was available so that the system would only be configured the way **they** wanted it to be. This is IT colonialism. Regions care about themselves first and foremost, and one region cannot trust other regions to perform solution design for them. At the site Software Decisions where single and multiple instances are costed, we have placed this disclaimer on the instance selection. *"An instance is an installation of the application. For instance, most companies will have multiple instances of ERP if they are global—each country requires its own financial system. Multiple instances can be quite positive as it allows the application to be customized for a particular environment. This factor, while related to user number, is treated in this analysis as independent of it."* In the vast majority of cases single instances serve the interests of IT, but not the business.

[43] *"...technical realists point out that many difficult technical problems must be solved before SOA can become the backbone for a new strategic architecture, including robust protocols for accessing the applications, high-quality integrated data stores and a sound methodology for managing the overall process. Researchers Ross, Weill and Robertson admit that most companies are in the early stages of a four-part transformation to SOA that may take many years—even decades—to realize."* — The Trouble with Enterprise Software

them to support it. On the other hand, there was a large incentive to **say** that they supported the concept, as is explained in the following article.

http://www.scmfocus.com/sapprojectmanagement/2010/07/sap-will-never-support-soa/

So before we go forth and accept a new marketing message (i.e., two-tiered ERP), let's analyze whether it makes any logical sense. It is not clear how two-tiered ERP is much different from the current practice, where most companies have several instances of ERP. Let's look at a few quotations that define two-tiered ERP.

> *"Two-tier ERP software and hardware lets companies run the equivalent of two ERP systems at once: one at the corporate level and one at the division or subsidiary level.*
>
> *With two-tier ERP, the regional distribution, production, or sales centers and service providers continue operating under their own business model—separate from the main company, using their own ERP systems. Since these smaller companies' processes and workflows are not tied to the main company's processes and workflows, they can respond to local business requirements in multiple locations."*
> — Wikipedia

Obviously companies are already doing this. The real difference is in the acknowledgement that a foundational characteristic—single instance ERP—is giving way to a standard approach of multiple ERP systems, not merely as part of a short-term approach, but as part of a **long-term** strategy. I would not have guessed that ERP systems had diverged so far from their original intent in this regard, as I tend to work for just one subset of enterprise software that is connected perpetually to ERP systems.

The multi-ERP strategy has been around for as long as there have been ERP systems. Yet IT analysts, consulting firms and IT trade periodicals that discuss the new trend of two-tiered ERP strategies, fail to bring up the rather important fact that a big part of the ERP value proposition **was supposed to be a single instance of ERP,** as explained in the following quote from an article in the *Sloan Management Review*:

> *"The concept of a single monolithic system failed for many companies. Different divisions or facilities often made independent purchases, and other systems were inherited through mergers and acquisitions. Thus many companies ended up having several instances of the same ERP system or a variety of different ERP systems altogether, further complicating their IT landscape. In the end, ERP systems became just another subset of the legacy systems they were supposed to replace."*

How can so many entities actively promote the concept of two-tiered ERP without even mentioning that it is in complete opposition to one of the original value propositions of buying ERP systems in the first place? Simply put, it is ignorance, amnesia, or a desire not to disrupt various forms of funding that they receive from ERP vendors.

The Logic of Cost Reduction for ERP

All of the above factors undermine a primary argument used to sell ERP systems: they **reduce** costs. After the ERP market had become saturated, the cost reduction logic "declined as a point of emphasis," because the vendors were now motivated to sell different types of software. I have noticed other previous changes in SAP's story line as well. Back in the late 1990s, before they had a supply chain planning system, SAP essentially told companies that supply chain-planning systems were unnecessary. Advanced supply chain planning systems were designed to replace some of the supply chain functionality in SAP R/3. They offered supply chain functionality not available in ERP systems, in addition to more advanced functionality. The argument used by SAP at the time was that this software was only of interest to a very small number of companies. However, after SAP developed their own external supply chain planning system, they **changed** their message, proposing that it was now quite necessary.

Business Cost Reduction

ERP systems were supposed to save companies money through the standardization of business processes. ERP customers generally accepted this without question. The quotation below provides an example of the pitch.

> *"It is also one of the most worthwhile initiatives for securing your place in a competitive market. A successful, enterprise-wide implementation will move your company from one with piecemeal business procedures and no overall plan, to a re-engineered organization that is poised to take growth and profitability to a whole new level."* — Why ERP is Vital to Productivity and Profitability

This is an example of a generic argument that proposes that businesses were somehow lost in the wilderness, lacking direction until—**POOF!** ERP came to save them from themselves.[44] The next quotation is a more sophisticated explanation for what is still a flawed appraisal of the situation.

> *"Many organizations have several different legacy systems that have developed over the years to meet their information needs for planning and decision making. Often there is little or no integration among departments and applications used by separate departments do not communicate with each other. This means that data has to be entered into each separate department of the organization resulting in data redundancy and at times inaccuracy. ERP systems can virtually eliminate the redundancies that occur from these outdated and separate systems. ERP systems integrate various systems into one and data is entered into the system only once."* — What Managers Should Know About ERP and ERP II

It's hard to fathom why these companies had not already created interfaces between their applications. As has been explained in both the *The Integration*

---

[44] Coincidentally, this also follows the narrative of a Harvard Business School Case Study, where a business is in shambles but is saved by a Harvard MBA who rectifies all of the problems with some outstanding management changes. Problem solved. In the standard case study, sometimes the MBA wears a cape, and sometimes not.

Logic for ERP and *The Single Instance Logic for ERP* sections of this chapter, not only are there many other applications that must be interfaced to ERP, but often multiple ERP systems must be interfaced to one another. Therefore ERP has not *"virtually eliminated the redundancies that occur from separate systems."* We have the same redundancies and the same issues, except we **have newer systems**. The previous quote seems to have been written by someone who does not spend any time on actual projects, because those who have work experience in this area have come to the opposite conclusion.

As far as systems being outdated, one of the major complaints of ERP clients is that their ERP vendors have stabilized the functionality within their ERP systems and are no longer innovating. This was **the same complaint regarding legacy systems and the reasons they were called outdated!**

Here is another quotation that contains more unexamined assumptions.

> *"ERP systems are based on a value chain view of the business where functional departments coordinate their work, focus on value-adding activities and eliminate redundancy. ERP can be a valuable tool for managers to improve operational as well as financial performance of the firm."* — What Managers Should Know About ERP and ERP II

This sounds great; however, how would the author know this? A lot of things "could be" but I have searched through all of the research on this topic and there is no evidence of this. In fact, the ROI is so low, that companies have had to **change their stories as to why they implemented ERP**, often turning to the equally fallacious argument that ERP improved integration in their companies (as highlighted in the quote below).[45]

> *"ERP systems replace complex and sometimes manual interfaces between different systems with standardized, cross-functional*

---

[45] As I was writing this book, I often joked with friends that following up on the many false statements made about ERP is like chasing a squirrel around a tree. As soon as one argument is disproved, another argument is presented in a chained sequence until you end up back at the original argument.

transaction automation." — The Impact of Enterprise Systems on Corporate Performance

I have to ask how current this observation is and whether it still applies, or whether it was ever true. This paper was written in 2005, but interfaces between systems do the same thing that ERP does, and have for many years.

The Logic of ERP Driven Improved Financial Performance

It is important to list this as one of the major logics that drove ERP purchases, however, because Chapter 7: "The High TCO and Low ROI of ERP" provides all the background information to understand how this logic actually turned out in reality, it made more sense to address it in that chapter.

Conclusion

This chapter covered the other logics—in addition to best practices and integration benefits that were used to sell ERP systems. All of these logics are similar in that they were over simplifications of reality, and none of them were ever actually proven true. They were never hypotheses that were formulated to be tested. They were proposals that were designed to help pave the way for software and consulting purchases. The evidence is clear that none of the logics were proven to be correct, and yet there is almost a total blackout of this fact. Academic research shows this, but exceedingly few have addressed the discrepancy between the official storyline on ERP and the research. Instead the logics presented in this chapter continue to be used in order to sell more software and consulting. This displays a concerning inability of corporate buyers to differentiate between evidence based statements and marketing propaganda. In the next chapter we will explain the total cost of ownership of ERP systems—which is directly related to the logic of whether ERP systems reduce costs.

CHAPTER 7

The High TCO and Low ROI of ERP

The Wikipedia definition of total cost of ownership (TCO) is as follows:

> *"Total cost of ownership (TCO) is a financial estimate whose purpose is to help consumers and enterprise managers determine direct and indirect costs of a product or system. It is a management accounting concept that can be used in full cost accounting or even ecological economics where it includes social costs."*

Background on TCO

We find TCO research incredibly illuminating. TCO is one of the most misunderstood, abused and underutilized tools for enterprise software decision-making. Our work on TCO has provided us with insight across multiple software categories. In fact, it is a **mistake** to limit the use of TCO to such a narrow range of decisions. Because we perform TCO for so many software categories, we know the following:

- How the TCO varies based upon the size of the implementation.

- How the TCO varies based upon the delivery method (SaaS or on-premises).

- How TCO varies based upon the complexity of the implementation.

- The average percentage that one can expect the implementation to cost for any one specific cost item, or for cost categories such as implementation, license, hardware, or maintenance and support.

- Using ERP combined with 100 percent ERP vendor applications.

- Using ERP combined with 100 percent best-of-breed solutions.

- Open source ERP, 100 percent best-of-breed solutions.

- No ERP, 100 percent best-of-breed solutions.

- The risks of various software categories.

The analyses include assumptions that are often not considered, such as realistic average implementation times. These implementation times, which are habitually underestimated by vendors and consulting companies, have been taken from actual projects. I can say unequivocally that from this database of knowledge we have been able to disprove many deeply entrenched concepts that drive IT decisions to poor outcomes. In our view, combining unbiased and highly detailed TCO calculations, along with an evaluation of comparative software functionality based on strong domain expertise, are two of the most important inputs to producing quality IT decisions. Unfortunately, this knowledge is not resident within companies, and ERP software vendors (as well as consulting companies and IT analysts) have not informed companies as to the true TCO of ERP systems; it takes work to do this analysis, and probably more importantly, the ERP vendors do not want buying companies to know.

Various ERP TCO Studies Versus Our Estimates
The study *What Managers Should Know About ERP/ERP II* estimates the costs of ERP software licenses to be between 10 and 20 percent of the overall TCO, which is higher than estimates by Software Decisions. While the software license cost of most application categories averages 20 percent of the TCO, we estimate 8 percent of the TCO of Tier 1 ERP software is due to software license costs. ERP implementations take so long, and have so much customization, and therefore, maintenance expense. So it's not that the software license cost is lower; the TCO

is made so much larger by the customization and implementation expenses that the software license cost becomes a smaller percentage of the cost in comparison. The book, *Control Your ERP Destiny: Reduce Project Costs, Mitigate Risks, and Design Better Business Solutions* considers a reasonable estimate of the costs of ERP software to be 20 percent of the total project budget. According to this book, software vendors provide their potential customers with estimates (as do consulting companies) that **consulting costs will be roughly twice the cost of the software**.[46] One independent source, called 180systems, actually estimates that consulting costs average 65 percent of the license costs (71 percent for larger customers and 59 percent for mid-sized customers).[47]

Below is a meta-analysis and comparison of my individual TCO analyses in this regard.

Cost Estimates and Comparison from Four Application TCO Analysis

Costs	Supply Planning	Production Planning	Demand Planning	Service Parts Planning	Average
Software Costs	11.0%	16.0%	9%	14%	**12.5%**
Consulting Costs	27.0%	19.0%	28%	25%	**24.8%**
Consulting Costs Divided by Software Costs	245%	119%	311%	179%	**213.5%**
Percentage of Total Six Year Costs	38.0%	35.0%	37.0%	39.0%	**37.3%**

*While the software vendor estimate of consulting costs holds true for my sample (although you can see that there is considerable variability), this does not correlate with our estimations **because other TCO estimations that we have reviewed consistently underestimate the TCO of applications**. Because license costs are explicit costs, they are the easiest to estimate, and thus the easiest to overestimate in relation to other costs.*

---

[46] And this is not even the lowest estimate for consulting costs as a percentage of the license costs.
[47] http://www.camagazine.com/archives/print-edition/2011/aug/columns/camagazine50480.aspx.

Estimations from other sources are all over the map. Some entities recommend a rule of thumb of 1:1 between license and consulting costs. The software vendor e2benterprise recommends a ratio of between 1:3 to 1:4. We worked backward from these numbers and found that the estimations on the software license costs are solid, but the ratio of 1:4 only estimates consulting; it does not bring the total ERP cost **even close to the estimations of the total costs of ERP**. Additional costs such as the vendor support costs, hardware costs, and ongoing maintenance costs are well known. It is difficult to see why so much emphasis is placed on the software and implementation costs while maintenance costs are left out. Hardware costs are barely worth mentioning as they represent a small percentage of the overall TCO, but estimated maintenance costs must be included in decision-making.[48]

On our Software Decisions website, we estimate software, hardware, implementation, and maintenance costs—both external costs and internal costs. The maintenance costs are incurred to keep the applications running, but also include maintenance of customizations. As 96 percent of ERP implementations require moderate or heavy customization, work is required to keep customizations up-to-date with new releases and to augment the customizations, and this makes ERP software maintenance a high cost.

An important aspect to consider when evaluating ERP TCO studies is that the consulting expenditures on most ERP projects are significantly over-budget, something that ERP software vendors *would not have included in their*

---

[48] The transition of hardware from main cost component to minor cost component is an interesting story. Up until 1969, most software was leased along with hardware. However, yielding to regulatory pressure, IBM unbundled software from hardware, which meant that hardware vendors could no longer block software vendors from the marketplace, and software vendors could arise independent of hardware. This is widely credited with "creating" the software industry. Now of course the software that is purchased is far more expensive than the hardware that it runs on, and on-premises software and hardware is purchased, not leased. Since then, continual advancements in computing have rapidly decreased the price of hardware, while the prices of enterprise software have increased, although with the arrival of SaaS, it is very likely that this continual rise in enterprise software costs is about to come to an end. The scary thing for the enterprise software vendors that sell more expensive software is that in our analysis of far less expensive applications offered by smaller vendors, there is often a gap between lower cost options and higher cost options. Furthermore, SaaS has the ability to radically decrease the costs of developing, implementing and maintaining applications. These cost reductions are dramatic and some of them passed onto enterprise software buyers.

TCO estimates. Generally speaking, a 100 percent success rate is assumed for implementations (strange, as the real success rate is far lower than this) when vendors estimate TCO for ERP and enterprise software. However, if the project goes over-budget or fails, the estimates provided by the software vendor do not apply, and neither do the Software Decisions' estimates. We have observed this as a problem in terms of how projections are performed and I explain this in the book *Enterprise Software Risk: Controlling the Main Risk Factors on IT Projects*. We are currently developing risk estimators for all analyzed applications; these risk estimates auto-adjust based on the application, the consulting partner used, and the stated capabilities of the company. The company can perform their own interactive analysis right on the Software Decisions website.

What is the TCO for software that is never implemented? I have interviewed for several projects (and worked on a few projects) that were re-implementations, where the software failed to go live. That failure may have taken a year and a half; the company focused on other things and then decided to re-implement the software **two and a half years after it began the first implementation**. If the software is taken live the second time, most likely the project will have a negative ROI. The standard ERP TCO calculators we provide at Software Decisions would not apply. Therefore, a question that anyone with an interest in ERP estimation should ask is: If 60 percent of ERP implementations fail, and if the vast majority of ERP *implementations miss their deadlines by significant durations*, why are TCO estimations still based upon assumptions that do not include these very critical factors? There is little disagreement on the fact that companies repeatedly underestimate the costs of ERP systems.

> *"In ERP systems, having clear criteria for success is particularly important since the cost and risk of these valuable technological investments must be reviewed in light of possible payoffs. Mabert, et al. (2001) put the total ERP implementation cost at tens of millions of dollars for a medium-sized company and $300 to $500 million for large international corporations."* — Measures of Success in Project Implementing Enterprise Resource Planning

According to Aberdeen, the average number of users per ERP software vendor is as follows (we used Aberdeen's numbers for this purpose, although Aberdeen's TCO studies were not used in this book):

Average Number of Users Per ERP Vendor

Vendor	Number of Users	Software Cost (2006 Study)		Inflation Adjusted for 2013		Cost Per User	
Oracle	440	$	1,159,091	$	1,474,687	$	3,352
SAP	385	$	830,033	$	1,056,034	$	2,743
Lawson	195	$	408,333	$	519,514	$	2,664
QAD	148	$	328,706	$	418,206	$	2,826
Infor	104	$	237,170	$	301,746	$	2,901

*There are significant price differences if just the aggregate license revenues are compared among a sample of ERP vendors. However, this difference in license revenue is primarily driven by the differences in the average number of users. On average, the Tier 1 ERP vendors such as Oracle and SAP have a much larger customer base, as measured here by the number of users. This relationship is so strong that a regression performed between just the number of users and the software cost results in a **96.75 R Squared**, as the following graphic shows.*

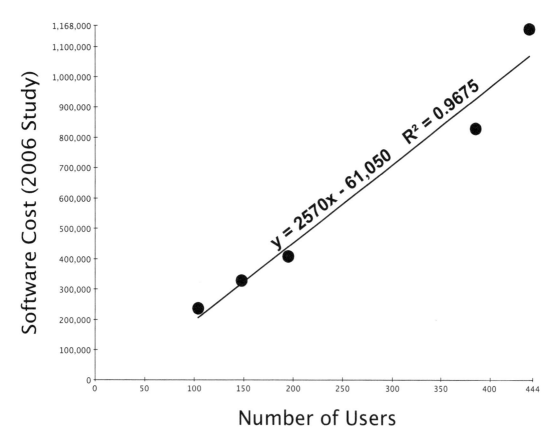

The average number of users for Microsoft is more comparable to Lawson, QAD and Infor than they are to Oracle and SAP.

Even though it is well known that ERP does not lower costs, the actual cost of ERP goes well beyond the direct cost of the software, but extends to the indirect costs such as the costs of maintenance, the costs of adjusting the functionality in other systems in order to make it compliant with how ERP works, to increased needs for customization, to losses in inefficiency as mediocre ERP functionality is used in place of better functionality that could be obtained by buying specialized software.

In the vast majority of cases, companies did not perform TCO analyses prior to purchasing ERP systems. It is now long forgotten that ERP systems were sold based on the concept that they would **lower costs** (the idea that an ERP system could have a low TCO is laughable even in the present day). Since then, ERP systems have proven to be very expensive, not only to implement but also to maintain, as the following quotation explains.

> *"ERP systems were expensive, too, costing companies more than they had ever paid for software when costs had been based on per workstation usage. But that price tag was dwarfed by the installation charges, because companies had to hire brigades of outside consultants, often for a number of years, to actually get the software up and running. While the average installation cost $15 million, large organizations ended up spending hundreds of millions of dollars."*
> — The Trouble with Enterprise Software

The long-lived mistakes with respect to ERP have affected every part of IT today. ERP systems have proved to be much more expensive than even the highest "generalized" cost estimates (even though 80 percent of the time companies did no real estimation), and ERP systems now consume a very substantial portion of the overall IT budget, particularly for companies that purchased from the most expensive Tier 1 ERP software vendors. The high investment in ERP negates investment in other possible applications, even though most of these other applications would have a higher ROI than ERP. All ERP ever offered was basic functionality, and any company that has basic functionality consuming the majority of its IT budget has a serious problem of resource allocation. By that measure, an enormous number of companies have this problem.

The direct cost of ERP systems has continued to increase. When companies give so many modules over to one vendor, they also give up a lot of negotiating leverage. The ERP vendors use this leverage to:

- Sell uncompetitive software in other areas of the same account.

- Increase the cost of the yearly support contract. The TCO of on-premises ERP systems is generally considered to be high compared to other application categories.

It is quite amazing that writers who cover ERP implementations do not bring up these issues with any frequency. Various articles will discuss how expensive ERP systems seem, but the enormous elephant in the room—the leverage of ERP vendors—is unaddressed.

Why ERP Equals Long Implementation Times

The implementation time for ERP systems is the longest of any enterprise software category. The term "implementation time" is laden with assumptions. At the SCM Focus companion site, Solution Decisions TCO, we perform risk and duration estimation for all of the major enterprise software categories. ERP has by far the longest implementation of any software category—and by a wide margin.[49] Furthermore, ERP software comes with high risks for implementation. According to IDC, 15 percent of survey respondents implemented their ERP software again. What was the implementation time on those projects? It is not easy to find detailed TCO studies on ERP systems, which is one of the reasons we began estimating it at a separate website.

ERP ROI

The ROI of ERP is an interesting topic; as one would expect, a company implementing an application with a very high TCO is put at a disadvantage when it comes to obtaining a high ROI.

> "A Meta Group study of sixty-three companies a few years ago found that it took eight months after the new system was in (thirty-one months in total) to see any benefits. The median annual savings from the new ERP system were $1.6 million—pretty modest, considering that ERP projects at big companies can cost $50 million or more. ERP systems may be integrated, but on-premises ERP has proven to be poor at integrating to other applications and to business partners."
> — The ABCs of ERP

---

[49] This site is available at http://www.softwaredecisions.org.

"Markus, et al. (2000) argued that the companies that adopted ERP systems need to be concerned with success, not just at the point of adoption, but also further down the road. After ERP implementation is complete, the expected return may not come as soon as desired. In fact, most ERP systems show negative return on investment (ROI) for the first five years that they are in service." — Measures of Success in Project Implementing Enterprise Resource Planning

This is quite a statement. And the implications of this statement cannot be understood without performing a little math.

ERP Timelines	Years	% of Time Company Receives "Some" Return
Average Implementation Time	2.5	
Five Years of Use	5	
Low Side of How Long ERP Systems is Used	8	
High Side of How Long ERP Systems is Used	12	
Years Company Can Expect Benefits from System (Low Side)	3.0	38%
Years Company Can Expect Benefits from System (High Side)	7.0	58%

The math presented above is problematic when one compares the known estimated durations with ERP. Generally ERP systems are thought to have a useful life of between eight and twelve years. If it is true that no return can be expected for the first five years of use, it is seven-and-a-half years into the ERP project when the company has begun paying for the ERP system (including two-and-a-half years of implementation time). If the ERP system is decommissioned after eight years, the company has three years to receive a return (which would clearly mean a negative ROI). If the ERP system is decommissioned at the high side (after twelve years), there are seven years or 58 percent of the total time the ERP system is in the company to receive a return.

While the information up to this point is problematic, the news gets worse with the following statement.

> *"After the first five years of use, a company can expect steady returns, but not in the traditional form of revenue. As Markus and Tanis (2000) indicated, different measures are needed at different stages in the system lifecycle and a minimum set of ERP success metrics should include projects metrics, early operational metrics and long-term business results."* — Measures of Success in Project Implementing Enterprise Resource Planning

According to this quote, there are close to no financial returns, which is what studies generally say. Researchers think that no return can be expected until seven-and-a-half years after the ERP project kick-off. While no financial return can be demonstrated, it is implied continually that ERP pays off in other ways, ways that are imperceptible to the company's financial health. In fact, the company may not be able to expect a return until other applications are connected to the ERP system.

> *"'There's a general understanding today that ERP is the investment you have to make just to get into the game,' says Josh Greenbaum, a principal analyst with Enterprise Applications Consulting. 'First you have to get ERP installed, and then you can take a look around and see where major ROI can be achieved. It's the so-called second-wave applications, such as business intelligence, supply-chain management, and online procurement, that can leverage the ERP backbone and offer the highest return,' says Greenbaum."* — Making ERP Add Up

That is one incredible statement. Talk about "future selling." The constant assumption is that ERP somehow puts a company in a better position to derive benefit from other applications, as discussed in Chapter 10: "How ERP Distracts Companies from Implementing Better Functionality." There is no evidence that ERP improves the benefits/return on investment from other applications; this is utter conjecture on the part of this analyst.

Then comes the other issue with estimating operational benefits, as the following quotation explains.

> *"According to Parr and Shanks (2000) 'ERP project success simply means bringing the project in on time and on budget.' So, most ERP projects start with a basic management drive to target faster implementation and a more cost-effective project... Summarizing, the project may seem successful if the time/budget constraints have been met, but the system may still be an overall failure or vice versa. So these conventional measures of project success are only partial and possibly misleading measures when taken in isolation (Shenhar and Levy, 1997)."* — Measures of Success in Project Implementing Enterprise Resource Planning

With such high costs, ERP ends up consuming a very large portion of the overall IT budget. The maintenance of ERP systems consumes anywhere from 50 to 90 percent of the IT budget according to Forrester and Gartner.[50] ERP software, as with any other type of software, consumes resources across all of the IT operating budget categories. ERP has proven to be an expensive proposition for companies, and did not reduce costs as was promised by its proponents. The problem is that both the direct AND indirect costs of ERP systems have been high.

The Low (and Misleading) ROI of ERP Software
It is difficult for ERP to have a good ROI if it also has a high TCO. Obviously, the TCO is the denominator in the ROI equation, with the business benefits being the numerator. Another problem with ERP ROI is that ERP systems take a long time to implement.

Other estimations are shorter, but I have not been able to find any research that provides a solid method for this analysis. I quote this book's estimate not because

---

[50] It's difficult to fathom how the upper limit proposed by Forrester and Gartner could be correct, because if it were actually 90 percent, then essentially the company could invest in nothing else. Perhaps this figure would apply to companies that have very few applications aside from their ERP system. If a company is in fact allocating this much money to their ERP system, it is a severe misallocation of resources. These would likely be smaller companies that were misled by Tier 1 ERP vendors and consulting companies into investing in an ERP system that they could not afford.

it explains or divulges its data points, but because I find the book credible in other aspects. However, even this book's estimates are lower than the study by Meta Group, which proposed that it takes eight months until the ERP system begins showing **any** benefit. This figure is contradicted by the study *The Impact of Enterprise Systems on Corporate Performance,* and that after the ERP implementation the company loses productivity every year the ERP system is live. (This study is discussed on the next page.)

If we take the lowest estimate and average the high and the low values, we get the following:

$$((12 + 36 \text{ months})/2 + (4 + 6 \text{ months})/2) = 29 \text{ months}$$
$$29 \text{ months} / 12 = 2.4 \text{ years}$$

According to the above calculation, a company must pay for an ERP implementation for two years and then wait another five months before the software is functional to the degree that it can be relied upon.[51] That is taking the average of the ***most optimistic of the three estimates***; other scenarios are not even *this* rosy.[52] For instance, one scenario is that the company never sees any productivity benefit even though it implements the ERP system. Another scenario is that there is a 40 percent likelihood of major disruption to business operations during the go-live. What is the cost of this "major disruption"? Well, that is not estimated. What about smaller disruptions? It would seem quite likely that smaller disruptions occur with even greater frequency; however, I have never seen a TCO analysis for ERP that includes the costs of these disruptions. At Software Decisions, we are currently working on adjusting the risk in TCO calculations, but do not yet have all of the data.

---

[51] But there is no evidence that ERP actually provides a benefit after this time has passed.

[52] Of course, other more optimistic estimates are available from the ERP software vendor or from a consulting company. However, it makes little sense to take any estimation from ERP vendors or from consulting companies seriously. Here is another explanation of the lack of reliability of these two information sources:

"Don't be fooled when ERP vendors tell you about a three- or six-month average implementation time. Those short implementations all have a catch of one kind or another: the company was small, or the implementation was limited to a small area of the company, or the company only used the financial pieces of the ERP system (in which case the ERP system is nothing more than a very expensive accounting system)." — The ABCs of ERP

Another interesting timeline was provided in the paper *Which Came First: IT or Productivity?* where a full timeline of an ERP implementation, as well as the software that followed it, was laid out.

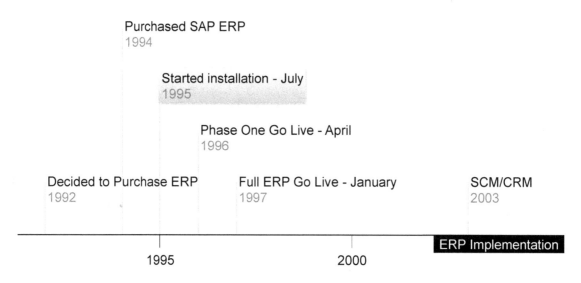

This shows the timeline for a relatively fast ERP implementation of nineteen months from the ERP system kickoff until the full go-live. However, this company would not have seen the full benefit of ERP until the ERP system was fully integrated, which is not mentioned in this study.[53]

In fact, most estimates are unreliable because they are put out there by consulting companies or ERP vendors themselves. Generally, what is not debated is that ERP software takes the longest of any software category to implement. Furthermore, most of the estimates of ERP implementation timelines leave out the time taken to integrate other applications to the ERP system. Gartner estimates that it can take up to five years to integrate the other applications within the company to the ERP system. Because the full benefits of an ERP system are not realized until ERP is integrated to all the company's various applications, the value realized is incremental up until that time.

---

[53] The authors created a graphic of this timeline, but I placed the dates into software I am familiar with in order to provide a consistent look to the timeline graphics in the book.

The Summation Up Until This Point

Considering all of this, it should not be surprising that research confirms the following:

1. ERP implementations show no positive business benefit, and often impose significant costs (e.g., missed orders due to lack of inventory, inability to ship orders that are received due to execution problems).

2. The potential for ERP implementations to show a positive business benefit for up to a year after an implementation is low, as the company is still adjusting to the radical changes that an ERP system imposes on a company.[54]

Once these problem projects are thrown into the mix, the average return for an ERP planning project is negative. While there is no research into the ROI of ERP software, one would assume that ERP would generally have a poor ROI for the reasons listed above. Others, such as the *Sloan Management Review*, have noted this lack of ROI research:

> *"Given the high costs of the systems—around $15 million on average for a big company—it's surprising...that despite such study, researchers have yet to demonstrate that 'the benefits of ERP implementations outweigh the costs and risks.' It seems that ERPs, which had looked like the true path to revolutionary business process reengineering, introduced so many complex, difficult technical and business issues that just making it to the finish line with one's shirt on was considered a win."*

This begs the question as to why, as stated in the above quote, *"ERPs...had looked like the true path to revolutionary business process reengineering."*

The answer to this question is simple: a number of entities with a strong financial bias declared it to be so.

---

[54] I included no software costs or support costs because I was not able to ascertain the costs of the SAP module. SAP's costs are variable per client. Of course the company would pay significantly for this module and then for the support. When these costs are included, my estimate would show a negative ROI for all of the SAP modules that I analyzed. This is explained in detail in the book, *Enterprise Software TCO: Calculating and Using Total Cost of Ownership for Decision Making.*

Negative ROI: The Missing Link of the ERP ROI Research
Every research study into the ROI of ERP systems that I reviewed (except for the research that attempts to find a correlation between ERP implementations and the financial performance of companies) contains several flaws. Some of these flaws have been stated previously in this book and relate to an underestimation of the TCO as described in the previous section. Obviously if the TCO is not conclusive, then the ROI is inaccurate; the TCO is the *base*, or the "I" in the ROI.

Let's review the issues with estimations of the TCO (issues that are usually overlooked) before moving on to examining the error from the return side.

1. The TCO for ERP projects are not adjusted for risk.

2. The total length of ERP projects is not included in the TCO calculation. The longer the project, the longer it takes for the project to pay back the investment. Furthermore, ERP projects are so problematic from the integration perspective that it can take up to five years for them to be fully integrated with other systems, and therefore fully operational.

3. There is a 40 percent likelihood of a major operational disruption after an ERP project goes live. The costs of these major disruptions nor the costs of smaller disruptions are included in the ERP TCO calculations.

4. ERP TCO estimations consistently underestimate the actual TCOs of projects. These estimations completely neglect or underestimate the costs of internal resources to adjust to and learn the ERP system. Actually this issue is not specific to ERP software, but is a feature of enterprise software generally. However, the large-scale nature of ERP software makes this issue worse.

The error on the return side of ROI is that ERP ROI studies look at the ERP system in **isolation from the other software that the company implements**. However, as will be explained in more detail in "Case Study #4 of ERP Misuse: Intercompany Transfer", the transactional inflexibility of ERP systems—the fact that they have their modules so tightly integrated—restricts a company's ability to fully leverage the functionalities in applications that are connected to ERP systems. As a result, a company with an ERP system will receive less value from other applications that they implement (unless the application is extremely simple) than a company that **does not** have an ERP system. Companies with ERP systems do not leverage the other applications that they purchase and implement, and this means the companies must use more of the mediocre functionality within the ERP system. I found this statement by Aberdeen very interesting:

> *"As ERP has become more pervasive, there is always a risk in perceiving it as necessary infrastructure. If viewed as a requirement for doing business, companies also run the risk of neglecting to measure the business benefits resulting from its implementation."*

I would say this statement is a bit late. The decision to purchase ERP was not based upon measurement of its business benefits, but was primarily based upon an idea that ERP systems were "necessary infrastructure."

Support Costs of ERP

The maintenance costs of Tier 1 ERP (and possibly other tiers as well) are likely headed upward. ERP software is stabilizing; it is falling further and further behind the other applications connected to it and that can replace much of ERP's functionality. Instead, SAP moves almost all of their newer functionality to their non-ERP modules, as they can charge new license fees for the modules. Analysts are not picking up on this, but investment in ERP has wilted, and ERP systems are unable to meet requirements without further customization. Your ERP vendor already has your ERP business; now they want to nudge up the ERP support costs and they have some other software they would like to sell you.

The High Opportunity Cost of ERP

The opportunity costs of ERP are underemphasized (or ignored altogether). The term "opportunity cost" is used infrequently, so let's define it before we explain how it should be used in making decisions:

> *"In microeconomic theory, the opportunity cost of a choice is the value of the best alternative forgone, in a situation in which a choice needs*

to be made between several mutually exclusive alternatives given limited resources. Assuming the best choice is made, it is the 'cost' incurred by not enjoying the benefit that would be had by taking the second best choice available." — Wikipedia

In general parlance, costs are often described as the amount that we pay for things. Economists look at costs quite a bit differently. Opportunity cost is one cost category, and sunk cost—something I will get into in Chapter 11: "Alternatives to ERP or Adjusting the Current ERP System"—is another.

Promoters of ERP tend to present any benefits of ERP without acknowledging that the time and effort spent on ERP could have gone into other initiatives. However, the gain from those systems should be compared against the gain from ERP systems.

Let's take a simple example. Imagine that I have no car. I have a hard time getting around town because I lack transportation. To improve my condition, I buy a Hummer. After a week, I report that I am able to get around town much more efficiently, and compared to walking, I am now much more mobile. Have I established that the Hummer was the best possible alternative? Obviously I have not proved this. I could have purchased any car—almost any of them with lower operating costs than a Hummer. Therefore, the question is not whether the purchase of the Hummer improved my condition compared to the other alternatives (these alternatives could have included any other car of equivalent or lower cost, public transit, bicycle, etc.). Does my analogy that a Hummer is the best automobile one can buy sound silly? Well it should, but it is no sillier, no less evidence-based, than the evidence presented for why ERP has helped companies. The comparison can never be between "something" and "nothing," but between two "somethings." People that compare something to nothing are stacking the deck in favor of the "something" and are not promoting research or a logical and serious framework.[55]

The Logic of ERP Driven Improved Financial Performance
Enterprise software implementations should have a positive ROI. This is why they are purchased. In this section I will provide a synopsis of the research findings.

> *"The results are based on a sample of one hundred eighty-six announcements of ERP implementations; one hundred forty SCM implementations; and eighty CRM implementations. Our analysis of the financial benefits of these implementations yields mixed results. In the case of ERP systems, we observed some evidence of improvements in profitability but not in stock returns.*

> *"The results for improvements in profitability are stronger in the case of early adopters of ERP systems. On average, adopters of SCM system experience positive stock returns as well as improvements in profitability."* — The Impact of Enterprise Systems on Corporate Performance

---

[55] This is also why so many "me-too" pharmaceuticals are approved. These are drugs that copy pre-existing drugs on the market (but with a slight twist to the molecule). They are not compared against the pre-existing drugs, which they emulate. Instead the copied drug merely needs to beat the placebo. Therefore, the pharmaceutical companies are never asked to show a net benefit over existing drugs in order to receive a patent, which they would not be able to do because they are essentially the same drug. This is explained by Marcia Angela M.D. *"Second, the pharmaceutical industry is not especially innovative. As hard as it is to believe, only a handful of truly important drugs have been brought to market in recent years, and they were mostly based on taxpayer-funded research at academic institutions, small biotechnology companies, or the National Institutes of Health (NIH). The great majority of 'new' drugs are not new at all but merely variations of older drugs already on the market. These are called 'me-too' drugs. The idea is to grab a share of an established, lucrative market by producing something very similar to a top-selling drug. For instance, we now have six statins (Mevacor, Lipitor, Zocor, Pravachol, Lescol, and the newest, Crestor) on the market to lower cholesterol, all variants of the first."* Pharmaceutical companies prefer to compare something against nothing rather than comparing a me-too drug against a pre-existing drug, especially to one that is often very close to identical chemically.

This makes sense because ERP functionality was more advanced in the past. Now the technology of almost any on-premises ERP system will be quite dated. Secondly, at one time an announcement that a company was going to implement an ERP system would have had an effect on stock prices because the system was considered leading edge. However, ERP systems are so common now that a bump in stock price can no longer be expected.

Interestingly, the improvement in financial performance for ERP lagged SCM implementations. When ERP is compared to other types of implementations, it consistently lags other enterprise software categories.

> *"The evidence suggests that over the five-year period, the stock price performance of firms that invest in ERP systems is no different from that of their benchmark portfolios."* — The Impact of Enterprise Systems on Corporate Performance

This means that investing in an ERP system did not impact the stock price of the companies in the study.

> *"The positive changes in ROA (Return on Assets) during the implementation period are statistically significant at the 5 percent level. Although the changes in ROA during the post implementation period are positive, none of the changes are statistically significant. Overall the evidence suggests that although firms that invest in ERP systems do not experience a statistically significant increase in stock returns, there is some evidence to suggest that profitability improves over the combined implementation and post-implementation periods."* — The Impact of Enterprise Systems on Corporate Performance

While the financial benefits of ERP investments are either nonexistent or barely perceptible, the results of SCM software investments were positive; while investments in CRM software were the same as ERP, they did not show gains. Furthermore, clients that were early adopters of ERP achieved better returns, which means that returns of companies that have recently implemented ERP are even worse.

"The results for the accounting metrics provide strong support that firms that invest in SCM systems show improvements in ROA and ROS (Return on Sales). Improvements are observed in both the implementation and post-implementation periods, with mean and median changes in ROA and ROS generally positive and most are statistically significant at the 2.5 percent level or better." — The Impact of Enterprise Systems on Corporate Performance

CRM on the other hand scores very similarly to ERP implementations: no relationship to financial performance improvement can be found.

"Over the full four-year period, the mean (median) abnormal return is –15.22 percent (–12.41 percent), and nearly 53 percent of the sample firms do better than the median return of the firms that belong to their assigned portfolio. However, none of these performance changes are statistically significant. Basically, investments in CRM systems have had little effect on the stock returns of investing firms. These results are consistent with that of Nucleus Research (2002), who report that 61 percent of the twenty-three Siebel customers that they surveyed did not believe they had achieved a positive ROI." — The Impact of Enterprise Systems on Corporate Performance

"Despite the generally positive acceptance of ERP systems in practice and the academic literature, other studies have not found overwhelming evidence of strong positive performance effects from investments in ERP systems. Our results are generally consistent with these findings." — The Impact of Enterprise Systems on Corporate Performance

"For example, although Peerstone Research (Zaino [2004]) found that 63 percent of two hundred fifteen firms gained 'real benefits' from adopting ERP, they also report that only 40 percent could claim a hard return on investment (ROI). Other ROI results are reported by Cooke and Peterson (1998) in a survey of sixty-three companies that

> *found an average ROI for ERP adoption of negative $1.5 million."*
> — The Impact of Enterprise Systems on Corporate Performance

> *"Overall we find that, controlling for industry, ERP adopters show*
> *greater performance in terms of sales per employee, profit margins,*
> *return on assets, inventory turnover (lower inventory/sales), asset*
> *utilization (sales/assets), and accounts receivable turnover."* — ERP
> Investment: Business Impact and Productivity Measures

This last quote sounds convincing, although no numbers are listed and there is no comparison of the financial benefit versus the implementation of another type of system. Furthermore, it is no longer possible to be an earlier adopter of ERP software; at this point one can only be a late adopter, meaning that the benefits to adopting ERP are lower.

The data for this report was taken from companies before or during the implementation (prior to the system being live) and prior to when the system is operational and providing benefits to the company. This same report stated that the benefits of the ERP implementations began to reverse **after the system was live**. Here are the productivity gains from the same study.

> *"There is a productivity gain during the implementation period,*
> *followed by a partial loss thereafter. When value added is used as the*
> *dependent variable, the gains are 3.6 percent during implementation*
> *with a loss of 4.7 percent for a net gain of –1.1 percent (t=.8, not*
> *significant)."* — ERP Investment: Business Impact and Productivity
> Measures

Conclusion

Did the information in this chapter shock you as much as it did me? When I first began researching these topics, I was also unaware that every one of the proposed rationales for the purchase and implementation of ERP systems would prove to not only be wrong, but spectacularly wrong. I found myself quite surprised that these false predictions had not been reported in some published form. A multitude of entities have misled readers as to the benefits of ERP systems. I don't necessarily assign a nefarious motive to all the people who have written about ERP vendors over the years. Certainly, vendors and software companies write marketing literature and have no interest in the truth. However, many journalists lack research skills and simply repeat what they have heard about ERP. Perhaps readers do not demand more, and if the journalists were to do the research, they might find things that would be unappealing and could cause blowback from their editors and advertisers.

CHAPTER 8

ERP and the Problem with Institutional Decision Making

The book up to this point obviously has interesting things to say about the decision making ability and software selection approach of companies. Decision-making in companies is often presented as highly rational. The assumption is that attentive and thorough research is performed before purchasing decisions are made. A perfect example of this line of thinking is presented in the following quotation:

> *"If IT were not delivering value, rational decision makers would not keep investing in it."* — Andrew McAfee

The above quotation provides an example of the logical fallacy of an appeal to authority combined with the logical fallacy of an appeal to accomplishment. The same argument could be made for exotic financial instruments. How could mortgage-backed securities and credit default swaps—which fell in value so precipitously that without government intervention every US investment bank involved in these instruments would have had to shut their doors—possibly be lacking in value?

Many entities, ranging from consulting firms to the business press that cover these companies, as well as the software buying companies themselves, have an interest in having this line of reasoning accepted. However, the results of my research and experience in software selection, some of which is encapsulated in the book, *Enterprise Software Selection: How to Pinpoint the Perfect Software Solution using Multiple Information Sources*, actually show considerable evidence to the contrary.[56] A few of the issues that are problematic for IT decision-making are listed below:

1. *Selecting Biased Information Sources:* Companies often lack the knowledge to make appropriate software selection decisions for themselves. Often this issue is not mitigated by hiring external parties because the buying companies are frequently misled by advisory firms. These firms are more interested in selling IT consulting services than in providing objective advice.[57] These advisory firms are not "fiduciaries," in that they have no legal responsibility to put their client's financial interests above their own. This issue is similar to the problem of a lack of fiduciary responsibility that the majority of financial advisors have, which is why financial advisors have a very strong tendency to place their clients into investment vehicles that benefit them more than they benefit their client's. This is discussed in detail in the following article:

   http://www.scmfocus.com/enterprisesoftwarepolicy/2013/11/09/
   fiduciary-liability-it-consulting-companies-have-no-fiduciary-duty/

   Enterprise software buyers rely upon research from entities that are themselves paid by software vendors, along with a host of other limiting factors.

---

[56] Secondly, because of politics and confirmation bias, after a company has made a software purchase, they will do whatever they can to justify the decision. The decision had to be a good one—after all they made it.

[57] Remember, we are told that companies absolutely must maximize profits and that all other things are secondary. The way that large consulting companies maximize their profits is by misleading their clients about the right software to purchase. The question answered in many software selection exercises is: Which application maximizes the profitability of the implementation for the implementing company? In my consulting experience, I have never seen any other question answered when a large consulting company makes their recommendations to their clients. However, according to the general thinking on the virtues on profit maximization, these consulting companies, while deliberately lying to their clients, are performing their proper function in the marketplace.

2. *Accepting Simplistic Explanations:* As will be shown repeatedly in this chapter, companies deciding which course of action to follow tend to be influenced by oversimplified rationales or logics. If the executive decision-makers knew technology better, and if they had studied the history of enterprise software sales methods, there is no way that the oversimplified logics that were so effective in selling ERP to them would have worked. Another way of looking at this is that it was simply all too easy.

3. *Companies Do Not Delve into Detail on Functionality:* There is a strong tendency for buying companies to accept that functionality between the software of multiple vendors is the same, as long as the description of the functionality is the same and the functionality is proven to be similar when demonstrated by a skilled pre-sales consultant. In fact, rarely is the competing functionality "the same." Often there are very significant differences in the usability, implement-ability and maintainability of functionality that is at first blush seen as identical across multiple applications. A purpose of the software selection process is to determine the best fit between the various desired functionalities versus its documented business requirements and the functionalities that are available from competing applications.

4. *Overestimation of Implement-ability:* Companies have a strong tendency to overestimate what they can implement. Software vendors that market a broad or deep set of software functionality are of no help to these companies. However, some functionality is tricky to implement properly. In addition, companies will often have a certain level of funding in mind for software implementations, but will then implement more advanced functionality that requires a greater commitment of funds than they are interested in making. This lack of funding, which increases the general failure rate on projects, is addressed with the concept of Maximum Tolerable Functionality, as explained in the following article:

   http://www.scmfocus.com/sapprojectmanagement/2013/08/maximum-tolerable-functionality/

5. *Susceptibility to Salesmanship:* Good salespeople are paid very well by software vendors for a reason. Salesmanship works. However, sales, regardless of how well done, does not have anything to do with how well the application

can be implemented. Software salespeople will become "best friends" with their prospects, but after the sale is made, the relationship will not count for much. In fact, salespeople frequently make implementations worse by insisting that overpromised capabilities can be met with "creativity." Some of the sales presentations that I have seen seem highly conceptual and have little to do with how an application is used in reality; one of the old jokes in this area is that the difference between a car salesperson and a software salesperson is that the software salesperson does not know he is lying. Unfortunately this joke has quite a bit of truth to it.

There is no way of getting around the fact that companies appear far less rational when one works within them and sees "how the sausage is made," than when one reads about them from afar. Business journalists, afraid of losing their access to information, have a strong incentive to place a positive spin on their coverage of a company, and most of the journalists are suitably compliant. Secondly, journalists don't actually work in the companies they cover; thus it is quite easy for them to get bamboozled. Typically the executives who are interviewed and provide information to the journalists are good at selling or at least good at making good impressions, and are motivated to improve their prominence in the field as well as to positively impact the company's stock price. A nice write-up on them and their company gives them even more negotiating leverage for salary increases, bonuses, stock options, etc. The most extreme example of this is the *Wall Street Journal*, which produces puff pieces on executives, building them into either geniuses or exemplars of highly capable and responsible corporate officers. The *Wall Street Journal* completely misrepresented how the industry worked when I was young and had not yet worked in these large companies. Now I understand the *Wall Street Journal*'s focus on making companies look good for stock market ends.

ERP Success and Failure

ERP success and failure rates are difficult to estimate, as was explained several pages ago. Much of this is definitional: what does one consider a success? The failure rate of ERP systems is far higher than generally understood. While some high-profile failures get released to the business press, in most cases the news simply never gets out. I know of several implementations that have featured very prominently in the marketing literature of several software vendors, and have been featured both by this vendor, and even at the implementing company for over ten years.[58] This customer is the main reference account for the software, has numerous press releases and marketing documents created for the project, and the truth is that the client is barely using the application. This is a case where the client has so much of their reputation wrapped up in the success of this application, that they cannot admit the failure—it is simply too embarrassing.

However, another reason that so many implementation failures go unrecognized is that companies often do not even know the applications well enough to know that their implementations have failed. I have written a number of articles that explain how some of the most advanced software available is poorly configured to such a degree that there was no point implementing the sophisticated software that had been selected.

http://www.scmfocus.com/supplyplanning/2011/07/09/what-is-your-supply-planning-optimizer-optimizing/

http://www.scmfocus.com/inventoryoptimizationmultiechelon/2011/05/how-costs-are-really-set-in-cost-optimization-implementations/

When I have brought up this matter to several of my clients, I have been told that there is no time allocated to fix the system; we must hit the deadlines to roll out the flawed configuration to new regions. At one company I was told that part of my role was to be enthusiastic about the system and to use my credibility with the business to get them to believe that the system was working well. The information I provide regarding a detailed analysis of system output and its fit with what the business needs is often suppressed and never reaches the ultimate decision-makers. The top decision-makers are in effect insulated from accurate information about how systems perform and instead are told only the good news. It's a complicated political stew of competing agendas that results in decisions being made without any logical foundation for the positives or negatives of the

---

[58] Following the currently accepted principle of releasing information appealing to the stock market, a company with failed implementations should not admit to this fact because the information may reduce shareholder value. Therefore, it is important to continue the façade that the software was successfully implemented. The company described here and I are both continuing to promote their implementation in the press, but are moving away from it internally.

actual impact of the decisions. However, I suspect that to those readers with significant work experience, this is not exactly news.

So the first assumption to dispense with is that because companies are big they must have rational decision-making processes or have effective channels for transmitting information to decision makers. This should help to explain why companies have universally accepted the following examples of logic for implementing ERP systems. I could speak at length on this topic and have written many articles that explain this in multiple areas, but that is not the focus of this book.

CHAPTER 9

How ERP Creates Redundant Systems

As I described in Chapter 2: "The History of ERP," ERP systems include very basic functionality for supply chain planning and management, sales, reporting, etc. Because this functionality is basic, many companies purchase and connect external systems to the ERP system. Let's look at the supply chain planning system as an example.

In almost all cases, during an implementation the planning system is **not** integrated to the ERP system's financial module. Instead it is connected to the ERP system's supply chain modules. In SAP ERP, the supply chain modules include all three of the nonfinancial modules: materials management, production planning, and sales and distribution. These modules then communicate with the financial/accounting module through the normal ERP workflow. This sets up situations where multiple systems are now used: both the ERP system supply chain modules and the supply chain planning system, leading to complex decisions as to what to perform where. These are some of the questions that I help companies with on implementation projects.

ERP as a Redundant System

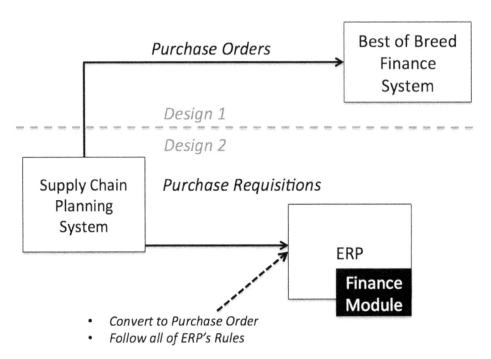

- *Convert to Purchase Order*
- *Follow all of ERP's Rules*

Ordinarily the external planning system could convert the purchase requisitions that it creates to purchase orders, and then send them to a financial system for reconciliation. In fact, by making the inventory management, planners, and procurement individuals use the ERP system, they are less efficient than if they used the external planning system, which is specifically designed for supply chain management. This same problem exists regardless of which type of external application is added—CRM, reporting, etc. The issue becomes, use the ERP system or use the external application.

When an ERP system is implemented, purchase requisitions must now be sent to the inventory management module in the ERP system. At this point, duplicate supply chain documents are created, and these documents must be kept in synch between the two supply chain systems. If there were no ERP system and the company had another supply chain application that it had purchased previously, the existing supply chain application would be decommissioned and the new supply chain application would be **connected directly** to the financial and accounting system. Therefore, the ERP system has just made the implementation more expensive and more complicated.

The Background on Supply Planning Database Segmentation

In supply planning, segmentation on the basis of the product-location combination is a way of dividing a database so that different rules can be applied to different database components. The standard approach is the following:

1. Place critical materials (those that are either capacity-constrained or that have long lead times—or both—or have a high profit margin) into the planning system.

2. Plan noncritical materials with the MRP, DRP and consumption-based logic in the ERP system.

The problem with this approach is that planners must use two systems (the ERP's supply chain modules and the supply chain planning system) to get the job done. A justification for this design is that the advanced methods available within the planning system would take too much time to run on the entire product-location database. This is a weak argument; simple methods can be run on product-location combinations within the planning system. In fact, any product-location can have a specific method assigned to it by simply assigning only the desired combinations of product-locations. All planning systems I have worked with (and I have worked with quite a few) have this capability.

Furthermore, some of the justifications for continuing to perform planning in the ERP system have really been about maintaining the relevancy of the ERP system rather than any real benefit to the company. In this way, ERP has arrested the implementation of more sophisticated and better systems. It's almost as if companies are continually attempting to justify the investments they have made in their ERP implementations. And of course, when the same vendor that sold them the ERP system is now selling them the bolt on the system, the vendor has the same predisposition: to help convince their customer that their ERP investment was a good one.

Finally, while the traditional approach is to convert planning recommendations (planned production orders, planning purchase orders, planned stock transfers) in the ERP system, it's actually very easy for planning systems, convert planning recommendations into execution objects (production orders, purchase orders, stock transfer). These execution objects could be integrated more easily to a financial application, cutting out the **redundancy of the ERP system**. Unlike ERP systems (at least, on-premises systems), the integration of these execution objects would be a simple matter if the financial application published to an integration standard.

CHAPTER 10

How ERP Distracts Companies from Implementing Better Functionality

In Chapter 7: "The High TCO and Low ROI of ERP," I discussed the opportunity costs associated with ERP. This chapter is related to opportunity costs but focuses on the distraction that ERP creates for companies that implement it.

Tier 1 ERP: A Philosophy of Putting the Mediocre at the Center

ERP sets up mediocre functionality at companies, and interferes with buying better software that could provide a great deal of value to the business. I will use several examples in this chapter to explain this prevalent feature of ERP software.

ERP implementations result in generic functionality being installed. Then, after the ERP system is installed, other applications that provide better functionality are frequently and selectively used to replace ERP. These superior applications must often coexist with portions of the ERP functionality that are still active.

The degree to which an application is integrated to ERP is a frequent topic of conversation, during which ERP and best-of-breed software vendors highlight their pre-built adapters, which connect the non-ERP system and the ERP system. What is left out of this discussion is the high overhead that many ERP systems impose upon the other systems that connect to it. Most people know nothing about how this ERP centric view of the IT infrastructure reduces efficiency, and simply accept it. This is very similar to the lack of thinking that comes to considering the poor productivity of Microsoft Windows. It's simply accepted.

The ERP systems rule the roost, and non-ERP systems are often measured by how well they work with ERP systems. But why should this be the case? The standard view is to place the ERP system at the center and to ensure that all of its needs are met. This book questions why this is necessary and if it is indeed even beneficial.

The analogy of a backbone or mother ship is **misguided**—primarily intended to drive an ERP-centric approach to the solution architecture. This philosophy never benefited companies, and deploying it will be increasingly disadvantageous as cloud computing becomes the norm. Companies that want to leverage the best offerings, as well as create the most effective internal set of enterprise software capabilities, will view the architecture as having no center, no hub. Rather, they will see all systems as providing some value and as being part of a connected ecology. A perfect example of this connected ecology is Rootstock, an integrated supply chain and sales application. Rootstock is part of the SalesForce platform and is pre-integrated to applications such as FinancialForce and the Fedex Shipping App.[59]

---

[59] There is also a UPS Shipping App.

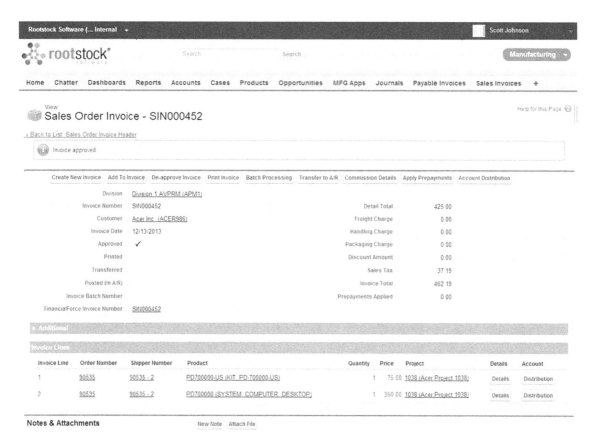

Here we are in Rootstock on the SalesForce platform. Now we need to create a shipment. We will do this "in" Rootstock, but will punch out to the FedEx Shipping App.

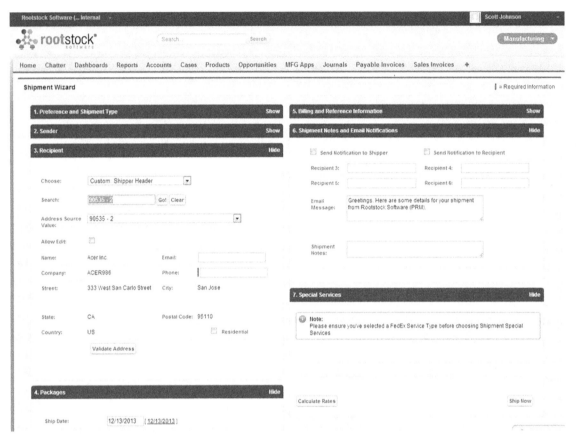

Generally applications in the SalesForce platform behave exactly like websites. One can punch out between various applications to leverage various functionalities. There is literally no "center." Currently SalesForce is its own ecosystem, which continually adds new software vendors. It is likely that this approach to enterprise software will become the norm.

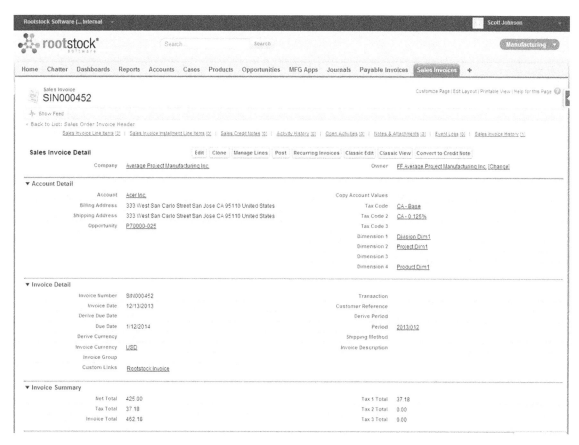

We will now check the invoice for this shipment, which again will be "within" Rootstock, but which will punch out to FinancialForce.

With the SalesForce platform, each application has to be configured to work as desired, but the customer does not need to spend time, money and effort to integrate the applications. Just this basic connection to the FedEx application would be, in the on-premises ERP world, a big accomplishment. First the ERP vendor would try to convince their customer to use their dated shipping application (sometimes this functionality is part of the ERP system, but sometimes it is part of another non-ERP product that the ERP vendor is selling). Then the vendor would grudgingly allow the external shipping application provider to connect to their system. Several months later the systems would be integrated—all on the ERP software vendor's terms of course. The SalesForce platform is not like that at all; it offers a far more efficient model. The platform offers pre-integration without any one application ruling the roost and declaring itself the center of the universe.

In the future, these integrations will be prebuilt by the software vendors and companies will be able to pick and choose (mix and match) the functionalities that they like. In this environment, it will be difficult for ERP vendors to lock their customers into mediocre functionality. This is currently the entire business model of the Tier 1 ERP vendors.

Choosing the Right Analogy

For on-premises ERP systems, a more appropriate analogy to the mother ship is redundancy. Once ERP is implemented, the system begs to have pieces of it replaced so that it can actually satisfy the business requirements—most often ERP is implemented only to be replaced in pieces. And once implemented, it develops its own inertia and its own defenders.

Tier 1 and many Tier 2 ERP implementations take time and resources that could have been used to implement the better, specialized applications. Many ERP systems have delivered low functionality in every area, and then set up the company to have more problems leveraging the superior functionality provided by non-ERP applications. Furthermore, the skill sets and orientation within the company becomes **ERP-centric**. Companies that use ERP systems typically become acclimated to poor functionality. No matter how limited the functionality, the response is commonly "well it's our ERP system." This statement seems to absolve the application from the responsibility of being a good system.

To explain how this works, I felt it important to provide concrete examples. Examples of four functionality areas follow, drawn from multiple areas ranging from bill of material management to intercompany transfer. I compare functionality in SAP ERP to functionality in specialized applications to show how stark the differences can be. These are just a few examples; I could write an entire book on how specialized applications beat ERP in most areas—and probably every area—of ERP functionality (I can't say for sure, as I have not evaluated all ERP functionalities). Each case study is labeled as "ERP Misuse," as the case study explains how ERP is often used, but how it is nowhere near the best solution.

Case Study #1 of ERP Misuse: Managing the Bill of Materials/Recipe

A bill of materials, or BOM, is simply a list of input items that connect in a predefined way to an output item in certain proportions and that takes a certain amount of time to be converted. BOMs are used for discrete and repetitive manufacturing, but not for process industry manufacturing. The BOM is one of the most frequently changed master data elements in the ERP system. As I will demonstrate, efficiently "managing" a BOM in an ERP system is impossible because ERP systems lack the full complement of fields that make up a BOM. Second, managing a BOM in a spreadsheet is problematic because spreadsheets are essentially sophisticated flat files. These are the two most commonly used tools to manage the BOM on the supply chain side of the business (design and engineering often, but certainly not always use a specialized BOM application). It is educational to compare and contrast the BOM to recipes and formulas, as this is one of the main areas of differentiation between discrete-repetitive and process industry manufacturing.

For discrete manufacturing (e.g., automobiles, toys and tools), the BOM relationship is between multiple input items and a single output item. However, in process manufacturing, where the final item cannot be broken down and converted back to the original input products (i.e., cheese cannot be disassembled into its original components, but an automobile can), one input item can convert to multiple output items, or multiple input items can convert to multiple output items. All of these relationships can be easily modeled in a spreadsheet. A recipe is the ingredients list. This is differentiated from the formula, which is the proportion and quantity of each ingredient to be added to make the final product.

I have one example each of a BOM and a recipe listed in the following graphics.

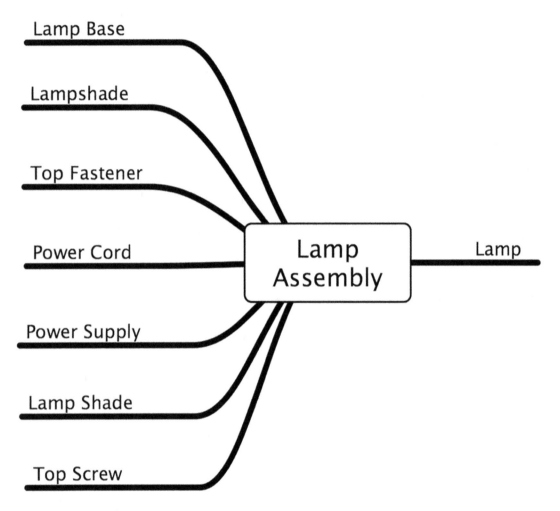

Here is a BOM. It has multiple input materials and a single output material.

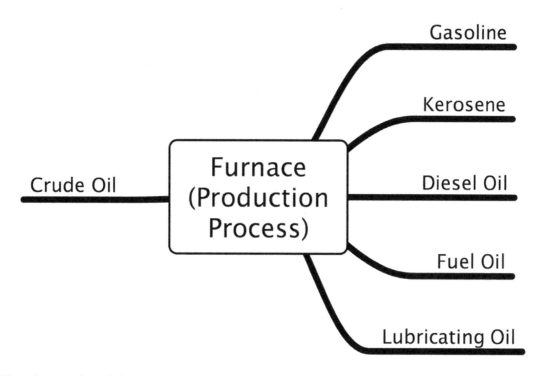

Here is a recipe. It has a single input material and multiple output materials, but it can also have multiple input materials and multiple output materials.

BOM/recipe management is often presented to executives as something that can be performed effectively and efficiently by the ERP system. While **never** actually true in the past, this is less true now more than ever as BOM management systems have developed rapidly over the past decade. For decades ERP companies, with the help of consulting companies, convinced their clients that the ERP systems provided functionality that was sufficient for managing the BOM. Unfortunately, few of these companies spent time examining the BOM functionality of ERP systems, and did not appreciate the reality that ERP systems are transaction-processing systems concerned with making, moving and accounting for product, and are not designed to meet the needs of design or engineering. By the time computerized systems reached design, the ERP system had claimed ownership of the BOM, which meant boiling down the very rich set of BOM/recipe functionality and fields contained within the design and engineering system to fit the limited ERP view of product data.

BOM/recipe management has yet to recover from this history. Most companies have nonintegrated product management systems, with Excel filling in the gaps. It is unfortunate because if CAD/CAM systems had predated MRP and ERP systems, the story could have been quite different. How far the supply chain and ERP functions have come in taking ownership of the BOM/recipes is reflected in the book, *Structuring the Bill of Material for MRP*, published in 1971. At this time, Plossl and others focused on making engineering BOMs suitable for MRP systems; the other uses of the BOM in the company were simply not a priority.

Exploring the SAP BOM User Interface

The SAP ERP BOM interface is extremely limited and can be shown in just a few screen shots. Furthermore, the SAP BOM functionality has remained relatively static since its introduction. The following screen shots will demonstrate that one should not count on manipulating or otherwise managing one's BOMs in SAP ERP. Rather, you want to do all the work in an external system and then simply populate the necessary fields in the SAP ERP BOM through an interface.

Display material BOM: Item: All data

Reference Items Subitems Long Text

Material	CH-1420 talyst (Grade A)
Plant	1000 Plant 1
Alternative BOM	1

Basic Data | Status/Lng Text | Administr. | Document Assgmt

BOM item

Item Number	0020
Component	CH-4110 Bag, 25 LB
Item Category	L Stock item
Item ID	00000002
Sort String	

☐ Sub-item ID

Quantity Data

Quantity	7	EA	☐ Fixed quantity
Operation scrap in %	0,00	☐ Net ID	Component scrap (%) 0,00

General Data

☐ Co-product
AltItemGroup ☐
Discontin. data

☐ Recurs. allowed
☐ Recursive
☐ CAD Indicator
☐ ALE indicator

MRP Data

Lead-time offset	0
Oper. LT offset	0
Distribution key	
☐ Phantom item	

In this screen shot, the item category and the quantity relationship between the output and input product is listed.

Display material BOM: Item: All data

🔲 🔲 | Reference items 🖨 👥 Subitems   📝 Long Text   ✂

Material	CH-1420	🔲 talyst (Grade A)
Plant	1000 Plant 1	
Alternative BOM	1	

Basic Data / Status/Lng Text / Administr. / Document Assgmt

BOM Item

Item Number	0020	
Component	CH-4110	Bag, 25 LB
Item Category	L Stock item	
Item ID	00000002	

Item Text

Line 1	
Line 2	

Item Status

- ☐ Engineering/design
- ☑ Production relevant
- ☐ Plant maintenance
- Spare part indicator ☐
- Relevant to sales ☐
- CostingRelevncy [X]

Further Data

- Mat. Provision Ind. 🔲
- ☐ Bulk Material
- ☐ Bulk Mat.Ind.Mat.Mst
- Prod. stor. location [ ]
- Prodn Supply Area [ ]

Some elementary fields such as relevancy of the BOM for costing, its storage location, etc. can be found on this screen.

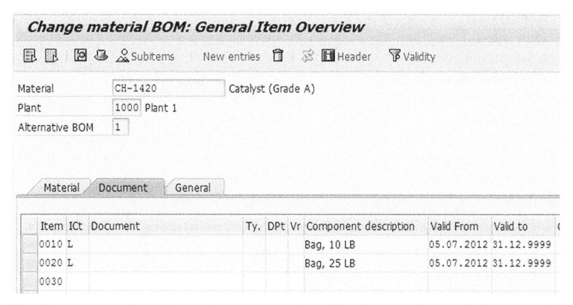

Here documents such as design documents and specifications can be attached to the BOM.

I have worked with ERP systems since 1997, I know the BOM in ERP systems to be an extremely limited master data object. Until I became exposed to the design and engineering side of the business, and began testing bill of material management applications, I, too, thought that the BOM representation in ERP systems was "correct."

In the SAP ERP system (called R/3 or ECC), the following fields are part of the BOM. However, itemizing the list this way provides an inaccurate perspective on how much information is contained in most ERP BOMs. For this reason, I have marked the commonly filled-in fields with an "x."

1. Material (x)
2. Plant (x)
3. Alternative BOM (x)
4. Item Number (x)
5. Component (x)
6. Item Category (x)

7. Item ID (x)
8. Quantity (x)
9. Unit Of Measure (x)
10. Operation scrap in %
11. Component scrap in %
12. Co-product
13. AltItemGroup
14. Recurs. allowed
15. RecursiveCAD
16. IndicatorALE
17. IndicatorLead time offsetOper.
18. TL offset
19. Distribution Key
20. Phantom item
21. Special procurement
22. Engineering/design (o)
23. Production relevant (o)
24. Spare part indicator
25. Relevant to sales (o)
26. CostingRelevancy (o)
27. Material Prov Ind
28. Bulk Material
29. Bulk Mat.Ind.Mat.Mst
30. Prod. stor. locatin
31. Prodn Supply Area
32. Validity to (x)
33. Validity from (x)

Some fields that do not exist in the design and engineering system are incorporated in the MBOM. The plant field is one example; the necessity to designate a BOM per plant creates more copies of the BOM in the ERP system. Furthermore, both ERP systems and external planning systems have the concept of alternate BOMs. This is clear from the Alternative BOM field in the listing above. Priorities are assigned to the alternate BOMs to allow the system to select between them.

The SAP ERP functionality has the following characteristics:

1. *Where the BOM Hierarchy is Displayed:* The association between all of the materials that are part of the BOM is shown in the BOM Material tab. The list is not indented to show the hierarchy of the BOM. The hierarchy must be determined by reading the description of the "component" or material that is in the list.

2. *No Web User Interface:* Internal employees design the user interface for access. There is no web user interface. In any case, because this data is used by the ERP system to generate its output, you would never want external parties to access these screens.

   The development for ERP or external planning systems is not focused on managing across the various BOMs. While it is always possible to write a custom report—it's not efficient when you can get this as part of the standard functionality of another application. Writing a report is necessary when you can't get the desired information out of the application—it's **not** a positive—although it is presented as a universal band-aid by those wishing to defend an application rather than objectivity represent its capabilities. Report writing is made necessary because none of the associative linking or cross-comparison functionality exists in SAP ERP. This is, of course, very limiting for the companies that rely upon ERP and external planning systems. However, a true management solution does all of this naturally as part of its basic functionality.

The fact that ERP systems are not a good system of record for the BOM is all true and undeniable for those familiar with BOM management options. And the BOM is only one example of data for which ERP cannot be the system of record. The quote below from the process industry software vendor AspenTech addresses another example.

> *"Further exacerbating supply chain issues is the fact that many companies rely on a complex mix of spreadsheets, enterprise resource planning (ERP) systems, and supply chain management applications*

*to manage their assets. While the ERP (system) is **typically the
system of record,** [emphasis added] supply chain technology
solutions often require data that is in a different form than what
the ERP contains, or falls outside of the ERP system entirely. One
example of this would be setups and transitions in the polymers
industry, which are typically not captured in the proper level of
detail, if at all, in the ERP system. Polymers producers are looking to
minimize time spent in transition from one grade to another, which
takes up valuable capacity of assets and produces off-spec material
that must be sold at a discount or on the scrap market."* — Key
Ingredients for a Successful Supply Chain

Regardless of how accurate the statement about ERP being the system of record
is for all enterprise data, I continually find myself reading statements in requirements documents on supply chain software implementation projects that are
similar to the following:

> *"Maintenance of data will happen in the ERP system as much as
> possible."*

This would be tantamount to reading:

> *"When traveling between countries, all employees should ride bicycles
> to reach their destination."*

Both statements are definitive, yet quite incorrect and quite prescriptive in proposing the worst way to do something. The second statement is only viewed as
more ludicrous than the first because of one's exposure level to the alternatives.
The reason I say this is that the exact approach outlined in the first statement
has been attempted in thousands of ERP implementations, never with good outcomes. ERP vendors that promise to bring "best practices" in all areas to their
clients recommend this approach. Can anyone really say with a straight face that
maintaining BOM data in ERP systems is a best practice? How about data that
exists in other systems, but does not even exist in the ERP system? Is that data
for which ERP is the system of record as well?

The fields that are available within SAP ERP were listed in this chapter to show how limited the BOM is within ERP systems. A constant problem with the term "best practices" is that it is often translated loosely into "whatever the software vendor has to offer." Exposure to the BOM user interface in SAP ERP should convince any person that maintaining and making changes to the BOM in SAP ERP is a poor practice. SAP makes the BOM difficult to understand and difficult to update. The interface was designed to enter information so it may be used by the system; it was not designed to allow the user to interact with the information. Furthermore, SAP ERP has weak search and associative querying capabilities with respect to BOM data. All of these issues generalize to other ERP systems, although many systems may have slightly better BOM interfaces than SAP ERP.

A good example of an application that can do all of the things I have pointed out as limitations with respect to ERP systems that I have described up to this point in the section is the application Arena BOM produced by Arena Solutions. Let's review some screen shots in order to see how the difference is night and day.

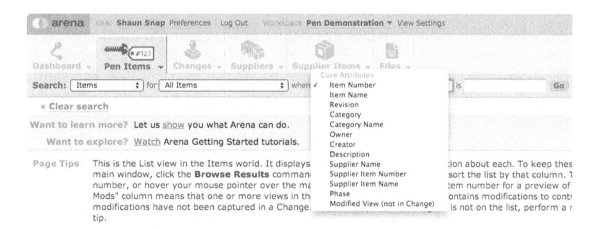

Arena can search by multiple criteria.

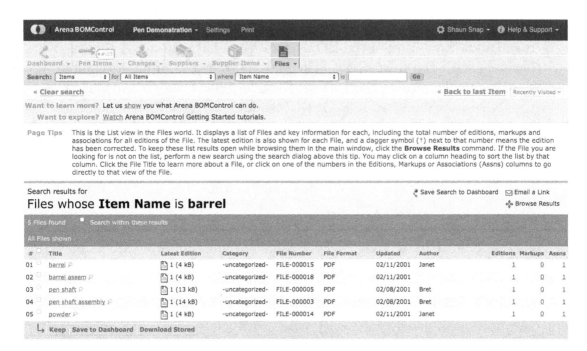

Here we searched for every item that had the word "barrel" in its item name. Notice that part names were found that did not contain the word "barrel." For example, when we check the pen shaft, we find that it is associated with the part that includes "barrel" in its item name. This type of association is very difficult to replicate in a spreadsheet.

Notice how easy these functions are when one has the right application. Tool selection is one of the most important decisions in any endeavor and decides the effectiveness of later actions. Companies are disabling themselves by so often choosing the tool that is lying around (i.e. the ERP system), rather than searching for the best tool for the job.

Case Study #2 of ERP Misuse: Disabling the Enterprise for Collaboration

While ERP systems connect to the other modules (thus allowing more collaboration internally), on-premises ERP solutions are extremely poor at facilitating external collaboration with suppliers and customers. Because ERP is an internally focused application and cannot collaborate within customers or suppliers, it must be connected to more software that provides specific collaboration functionality. For instance, the SAP application Supplier Network Collaboration (SNC) connects these entities to SAP's external planning application, which then connects to SAP ERP. If companies choose not to use this application, they can use an application such as E2Open. However, the results of collaboration implementations have been quite poor, and the fact that ERP is such an internally oriented application is a major reason for collaboration failures. The following article outlines the shortage of collaboration success stories.

http://www.scmfocus.com/supplychaincollaboration/2010/06/where-are-the-supply-chain-collaboration-success-stories/

The standard collaboration model is explained in the following graphic:

Standard Collaboration Model

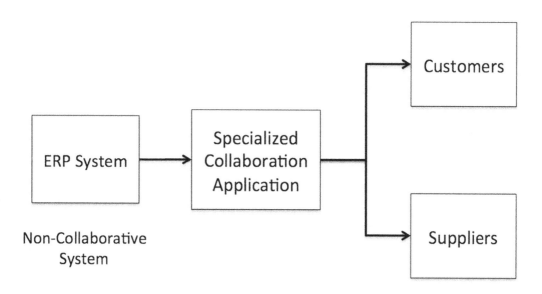

The standard approach outlined above is a specialized application that "just does collaboration," but what do companies have **to show** for following this approach?

In Tier 1 and Tier 2 ERP systems, collaboration is caught in a time warp with electronic data interchange (EDI) being the most common method of collaboration. EDI was a nice achievement decades ago, but it is a very restrictive way of collaboration as explained in the following article.

http://www.scmfocus.com/scmhistory/2013/08/earliest-edi/

Shouldn't all applications simply be collaborative? Philosophically ERP developed to automate and improve the productivity of internal transactions; however, its popularity has allowed it to set the agenda with a strong delineation between what is **inside and outside** the company, and this colors the software design approach of software vendors. However, companies are not structured as simply as they once were. Some companies perform design but prefer to subcontract out manufacturing to contract manufacturers that aggregate production from many high tech OEMs (original equipment manufacturers). Other OEMs outsource both their manufacturing and distribution. While all companies must collaborate, these companies perform what would have only been considered **pieces** of what companies previously did, have to collaborate like nothing before.

A company like SAP must be able to convince companies that collaboration is a specialized area—that no applications within the enterprise should collaborate outside of the "collaboration" application. How convenient, as they are selling dated applications that cannot collaborate!

My research for the book, *SuperPlant: Creating a Nimble Manufacturing Enterprise with Adaptive Planning Software* provided significant evidence that these inflexible delineations must be eliminated in order to create the collaborative environments that companies need to thrive. I quote from that book:

> *"Unfortunately for many implementing companies, this is increasingly*
> *where requirements are going, meaning that many supply and*
> *production planning systems are out of date with these requirements.*
> *This mirrors the problems that have plagued software vendors*
> *with respect to collaboration requirements. As with the treatment of*

locations, the treatment of collaboration in the design of most supply chain planning applications has been poorly conceived."[60]

The initial reaction to the above is that this transition would cause extensive security issues. I offer the example of the software vendor Arena Solutions.

Allowing Intelligent Input from Supply Chain Partners

A major selling point of Arena Solutions' software is the ability for partners to interact with and make adjustments to data for which the partners are subject matter experts.

For collaboration it is necessary that the application be very capable in regard to authorization: controlling who (both inside of the company and users working for companies with whom the primary company collaborates) can do what in the application. While SAP's internal authorization model is robust, it is difficult and expensive in terms of resource time to configure, and greatly lags behind Arena Solutions' authorization model. Of course SAP ERP does not have to worry about controlling access for external users, because they are not allowed in SAP ERP through the SAPGUI. But collaborative applications must have this capability. Even though SAP is the largest and best-known enterprise software vendor and Arena is relatively unknown outside of PLM/BOM management circles, the smaller software vendor thoroughly outclasses the large software vendor's security model. Conceptually SAP provides a security model that is from a previous era, when systems only had to worry about internal users.

In other applications like Rootstock, a large amount of collaboration is allowed internally, such as with Chatter, which essentially enables interaction via blogging style commenting on a wide variety of objects and is a standard functionality across all applications in the SalesForce App Exchange.

---

[60] This topic is related to collaboration design in software, which is barely discussed. It is covered in the following article: http://www.scmfocus.com/supplychaincollaboration/2013/07/why-must-specialized-supply-chain-collaboration-applications-exist/.

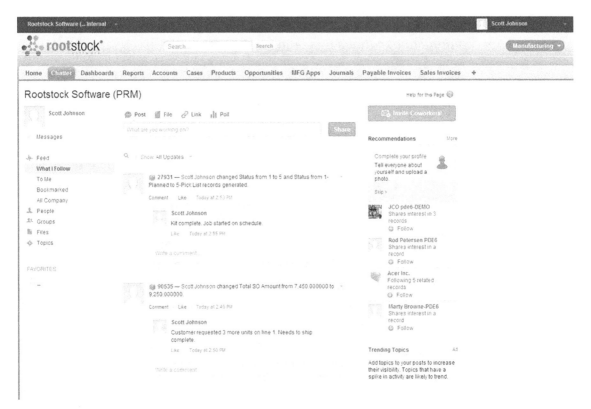

Chatter allows for better collaboration among users within the company. At a glance, one can see inputs from many different individuals and then can add one's own comments.

Outsourced manufacturing (one subcategory of outsourcing that can apply to non-manufacturing activities such as information technology) and contract manufacturing have been very strong trends over the past few decades. Contract manufacturing can be seen as an extreme form of supplier collaboration. In a normal customer-supplier relationship, the product is handed off between the companies. But in contract manufacturing, the subcontractor in effect becomes a part of the company, and, from concept through to manufacturing, the process requires collaborative input from both the customer and the supplier as if they were one company. In Arena Solutions, users can manage any level of interaction between the suppliers and a company, whether the supplier is an ancillary supplier that only supplies a few small value parts or a full contract manufacturer.

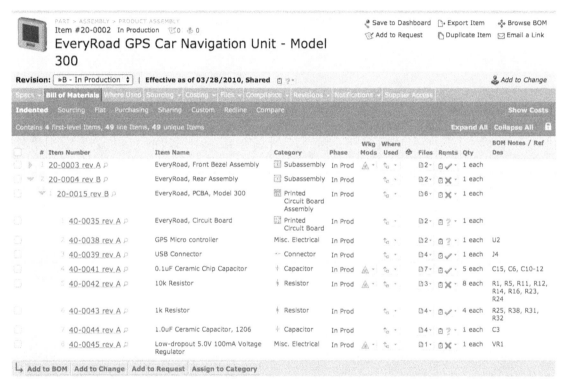

Arena can provide access to any external partner to any component of a BOM, without giving them access to the entire BOM. This allows OEMs to interoperate very efficiently with any supplier anywhere.

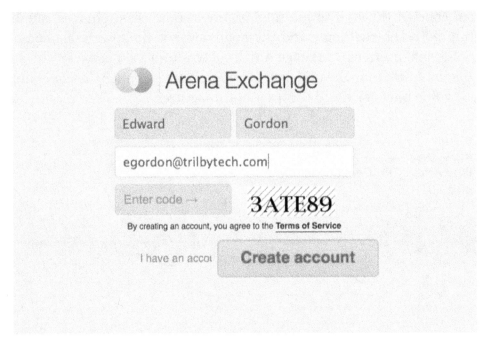

Arena Exchange allows a company to collaborate on components within the BOM with suppliers. Suppliers can self-administer if they have received an invite to create their own passwords.

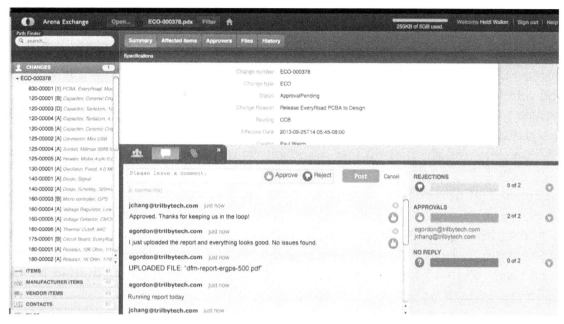

Once inside, suppliers, as well as everyone else with access, can collaborate in real time, see approvals, and read comments from all other users.

This brings up the topic of whether companies that do no manufacturing even need an ERP system, as the following article discusses.

http://www.scmfocus.com/erp/2013/10/20/does-a-company-that-performs-no-manufacturing-and-no-distribution-require-an-erp-system/

Case Study #3: How ERP Undermines Internal/External Planning

ERP systems were developed with a strong delineation between supply chain partners and customers. Since then, that delineation has blurred significantly. While ERP systems have been updated since they were first introduced, updating an old design in an attempt to meet requirements it was **never** designed to meet is quite a bit different than if the software was designed from the beginning to work a particular way. Subcontracting, contract manufacturing, direct sales through the Internet, modeling supplier capacity, supplier collaboration—all of these features blur the line as to what is inside or outside of the company.

Let me provide an example. In ERP systems, suppliers are external locations and resources cannot, at least with most ERP systems, be created or exist in supplier locations. Under the ERP design, suppliers are simply for accepting purchase orders. But what if a company wants to model supplier capacity? That is, what if the company wants to perform capacity constraining so as to treat the external location partially as an internal location?[61] Some planning systems can do this but the ERP system cannot, meaning that there is an inconsistency between the ERP system and the planning system that requires work to overcome.

Let us look at another example. Some time ago I received two packages from my favorite running store, RoadRunnerSports.com. I noticed that both packages were not from Road Runner Sports' distribution center, but separate, one from each manufacturer. I needed to send both packages back, but did not know where to send them: to Road Runner Sports or to the manufacturer's distribution center addresses, which were listed on the boxes.

When I called they told me that all returns come to them. I asked if this was a change in policy—did they no longer fulfill their orders? They told me that they used drop shipping for some items but not others, which allows them to provide a larger selection on their website. They stock high volume items at their DC. This is consistent with Amazon's approach, which is to fulfill some, but not all of the orders from their website (Amazon has grown into a marketplace where other online retailers also offer products).

---

[61] Some OEM's attempt to actively plan their CM/subcontract suppliers. This can work when the OEM is a sizable part of the demand of the CM/subcontractor (and there are still complications in this; a detailed explanation of the type of software that can easily handle this requirement is covered in the SCM Focus Press book, *SuperPlant: Creating a Nimble Manufacturing Enterprise with Adaptive Planning Software*). If a company represents only a small fraction of the demand of a CM/subcontractor's capacity, it makes little sense to model this plant. In fact, it is highly unlikely the CM/subcontractor would be willing to share capacity information; it's simply not worth their time.

What Changed and Who Must Know What

The old model for order fulfillment is from a time when most orders were fulfilled at a physical store. However, with ordering taking place on the Internet, it is not particularly relevant who fulfills the order, as long as it gets done. Amazon was one of the first web retailers to pick up on this fact and now it is a major part of their business.

Other online retailers are clearly copying Amazon's approach. A variety of system adjustments are required to pull this off. The less your systems are designed to do this model of order fulfillment, the more custom work is required.

This product is sold on Amazon's website, but the options below are actually fulfilled by someone else. Under this model, the sales order goes from Amazon to the fulfillment company, and the product goes from the fulfillment company to the customer. Payment goes to Amazon, which then pays some of this money to the fulfillment company. This is one example of how the traditional roles are changing.

Road Runner Sports must know the inventory position at their fulfillment company so that they know what they can commit to the customer and what is available to ship. Also, notice that the return does not go back to the fulfillment company, but goes to Road Runner Sports, which sends bulk returns to the fulfillment company. Increasingly, what is inside and outside the company is blurred, yet in the ERP model, inventory is shown for internal locations only. The problem is that ERP's model won't work for this business requirement.

Examples of the blurring distinction between what is inside and outside of a company are covered in detail in the SCM Focus Press book, *Superplant: Creating a Nimble Manufacturing Enterprise with Adaptive Planning Software*, which covers multi-plant planning, multi-sourcing and subcontracting. Superplant is the more accurate modeling of location interdependencies for production and supply planning that is provided by standard advanced planning functionality. Superplant alters the assumptions along which a planning system makes decisions. It can see relationships that software lacking these functionalities cannot access. Superplant allows for manufacturing processes to be planned and integrated across plants. Sources of supply are automatically and dynamically selected based upon changing circumstances, and the integrated planning of external partner plants are treated as if they were internal plants. These functionalities are logically grouped under Superplant as they all relate to improving the scope of planning with respect to how locations are treated when solving a combined supply and production problem. Superplant is characterized by an expansive and integrated view of planned locations, the ability to nimbly react to changes in things such as capacities, and to redirect to other sources of supply. **Superplant is not a management technique**. It is a specific set of software capabilities that must be configured, tested and accounted for in a range of areas from user training to integration to ERP systems.

For example, with some special multi-plant planning software, companies can leverage more of their manufacturing resources as part of the natural output of the planning system (that is without any manual intervention).

ERP Repeatedly Getting in the Way

In case after case, ERP systems, because of their introverted nature and dated designs, put up substantial barriers to flexibility when locations in a supply network are pseudo internal. Most vendors that sell add-on software don't spend much time or energy criticizing how ERP systems slow the implementation of their applications, but their implementations are, in fact, slowed. This is because all systems must be made to integrate back to a system that sees strong delineations between "inside" the company and "outside" the company. The very integration between the supply chain modules and the financial modules of ERP systems have made companies that much less adaptable.

Case Study #4 of ERP Misuse: Intercompany Transfer

Intercompany transfers are another example of the inflexibility that arises when the supply chain management system is too tightly integrated to the finance system (or more specifically, when an inflexible supply chain system with a limited ability to account for transactions in multiple dimensions is tightly integrated to a finance system). That will be explained in few paragraphs, but let's begin by analyzing intercompany transfers.

I selected the example of an intercompany transfer because it is quite good at demonstrating a transaction that has **multiple dimensions**. The content of the next few pages is some of the more complex in the book, but is necessary to understanding how limited ERP systems can be versus real-life business requirements. Secondly, while ERP proponents claim that business processes can be generalized, in the real world, requirements are becoming more complex, not less complex. Not being able to meet these complex and unique requirements has quite significant business costs. Certainly not every transaction is as complex as an intercompany transfer; however, having just a few complex transactions, which the ERP system cannot handle, can consume an extremely large amount of time.

Intercompany Transfer

An intercompany transfer is when a company buys product from "itself." While companies make a big deal about being global (and many certainly operate globally), when it comes to finance, a company must actually be incorporated in every country in which it operates, and must report to the tax authorities based upon its activities within a country. Thus, when a product (or service—but as this is planning we concern ourselves with products) is sent/sold between two different companies—say an automotive component from Toyota Japan to Toyota U.S.—an accounting transaction must be generated to record that the product has been transferred. This transaction, which is dated and has a transfer price, moves the product from Toyota Japan's "books" to Toyota U.S.'s "books."

If you search for the term "intercompany transfer" in Google or on Amazon, you will find that most publications on the topic of intercompany transfer are on the topic of intercompany transfer **pricing**. While accounting transactions are not particularly "relevant" for supply chain movements, they do have to be accounted for so that the supply network design can support the type of activities required on the accounting side. Supply chain planning systems and ERP systems generally have a standard workflow for dealing with intercompany movements, and this will work for simple intercompany transfers. However, as soon as the intercompany transfer becomes even slightly more complex, ERP systems most often require expensive customization. Furthermore, because of the rigid design of ERP systems, this customization will consume many analytical and development hours.

Intercompany Transfer Alternatives

There are two basic ways of handling intercompany transfers: a billing stock transfer order and a standard stock transfer order. A standard stock transfer order (STO) is used between locations that are part of one company code. With a standard STO, no billing document is necessary because the STO is an internal movement. A billing STO combines the document used for internal company movements with the invoicing aspect of a purchase order. This is shown in the following graphic.

Normal Stock Transfer

No Invoicing

A normal stock transfer, transfers goods between two internal locations without any billing.

A billing STO simply performs the same movement, and then performs the intercompany transfer in the ERP system. This is shown in the graphic below:

Simple Inter-company Transfer

Invoicing

Intercompany transfer is covered by standard ERP system functionality. It combines an internal movement with billing, hence the "billing-STO." Billing STOs work for straightforward intercompany transfers. The billing STO is the most straightforward way of transitioning ownership between two **companies within**

one global company. However, it does not even come close to meeting all of the requirements of an intercompany transfer. For instance, some companies have multiple locations that interact with one another during an intercompany movement; while the billing relationship is between two locations, the goods are moving between different locations. Entities other than the receiving location can be involved in invoicing the sending location. In fact, there can be four or five locations (or possibly more, although I have never seen more than five location interactions). The standard billing STO will not meet the requirement because the billing **is not applied to the location that is sending the product**. This is a complexity that is missed by those who propose the non-billing STO for every intercompany transfer situation. (I know as I used to be one of those who proposed the non-billing STO for a company that had a more complex need than I first understood.)

Matching Purchase Order/Sales Order for Asymmetrical Intercompany Transfers

To understand this nonstandard approach to intercompany transfer, we will begin by reviewing the standard purchasing goods transfer.

Standard Purchasing

Standard purchasing transfers goods from an external location to an internal location with billing. However, intercompany transfer combines features of both the internal stock transfers and purchasing.

Asynchronous
Inter-company Transfer

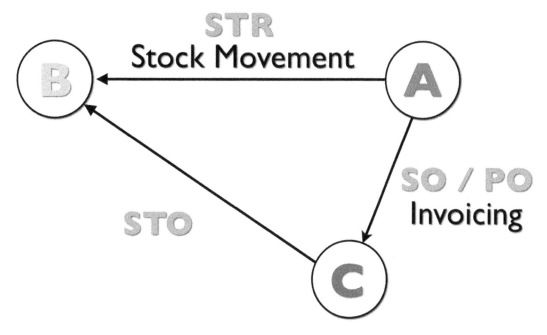

When the interaction between the locations is complex, and there are more than two locations, customization is required. Here the stock transfer goes between locations B and A, but the invoices go between locations A and C.

Custom Conversion Program

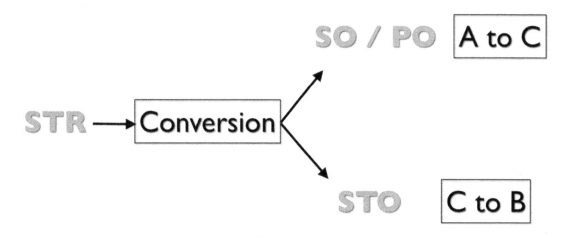

A custom program is required to take a stock transport requisition (STR), which in this case is created in the external supply chain planning system, and convert it into several documents, such as the Sales Order and Purchase Order pair between locations A and C, and the STO between locations C and B.

Thus, while an STR is created in APO, once it is sent to ERP, that same transaction becomes a purchase order and sales order (which cancel each other out as they are for the same item or items and same quantities. The sales order and purchase order are simply two transactions moving within a company, or should I say two different companies—a company buying and selling to itself but situated in different countries). Let's review how the two different approaches work.

1. *Standard Intercompany Transfer:* When product flows from an intercompany location A to location B and the invoice flows from location B to location A, a billing STO is the standard and most direct way of managing the relationship between the locations. The external supply chain planning system is

unaware that the STO is billing or not billing. Billing is managed completely in the ERP system as external supply chain planning systems do not deal with money. This approach is relatively easy to configure.

2. *Asymmetrical Intercompany Transfer:* When more than two locations are involved in the stock transfer relationship, the billing STO is not the way to set up this relationship, as it will place the invoice on the wrong location. In this case an STR is still created within the external supply chain planning system between the sending and receiving locations. However, once this STR is sent to the ERP system, the STR must be converted to matching purchase orders and sales orders. These items will move between additional locations beyond the two that are involved in the stock transfer.

A company involved in broad-scale international stock movements will sometimes have different intercompany transfer models. Some of these models mean the creation of a paired purchase order and sales order from a stock transport requisition/order created in the external supply chain planning system. Other movements may require no sales order, and in this case the STO is simply converted into a purchase order.

Controlling Transfer of Ownership in ICO Movement

In most cases, the transfer of ownership will occur when the product is receipted into the receiving location. Although this is the standard workflow for most ERP systems, **it does not meet the requirements of all companies**. Some companies want the ownership transfer to occur after the product has left the sending location but before it arrives at the destination location. I have found this to be true particularly of transfers with very long lead times, such as ocean carriage. The graphic on the following page shows the standard transfer of ownership versus the custom alternative.

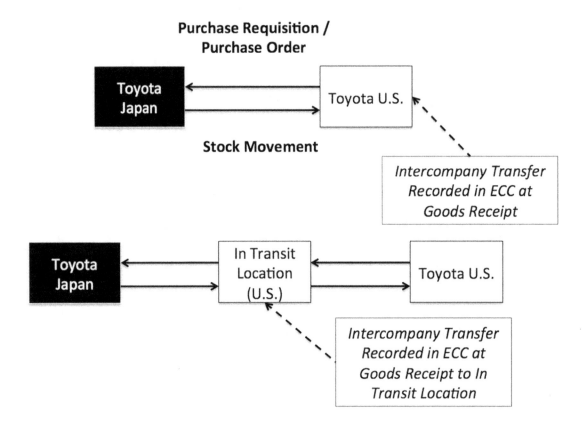

**Purchase Requisition /
Purchase Order**

Toyota Japan — Toyota U.S.

Stock Movement

*Intercompany Transfer
Recorded in ECC at
Goods Receipt*

Toyota Japan — In Transit Location (U.S.) — Toyota U.S.

*Intercompany Transfer
Recorded in ECC at
Goods Receipt to In
Transit Location*

The first alternative is preferable as it is in line with how many external supply chain planning systems and the ERP system operate. However, for different reasons, some companies prefer the second alternative. Because the transfer cannot be performed while the product is in-transit, an intermediate location—which is not an actual physical location but is a virtual location—is sometimes set up in order to perform the transfer.

The Core Problem of Limited Dimension Transactions

The issue that companies face when attempting to manage complex requirements of this type is that the ERP system is too limited and too inflexible to be adjusted. Instead of prescribing a limited set of functionality, ERP systems could have been designed quite differently. We use the terminology of STO, non-billing STO, and billing STO. All of this terminology really **just describes transactions that**

behave differently in a dimension where the transaction impacts the ERP system, as shown in the graphic below:

Transaction Dimensions

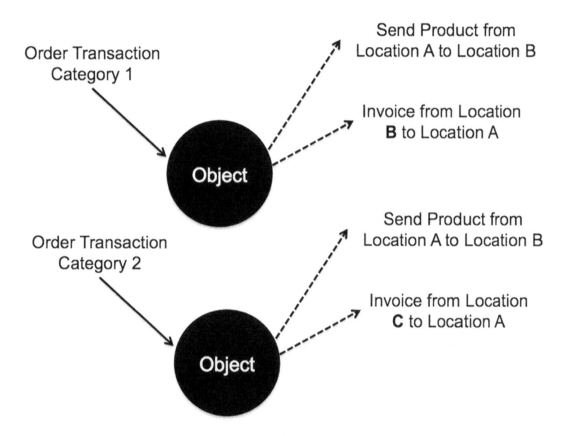

A transaction is nothing more than a container that initiates a series of related transactions—which change the state of the ERP database in prescribed ways.

Rather than prescribing a limited number of ways that a transaction can behave in a particular dimension, one can open up the options, and this can be accomplished with far less complexity and without the confusing terminology. It is unclear why so many ERP systems took such a prescriptive approach when developing the software in the first place. Perhaps they lacked the development sophistication to make flexible systems and wanted to reduce the costs of development. Creating a system of more limited behavior within the dimensions of a transaction saved development effort and money in the short term, but is ultimately a poor trade-off. The software must be customized per client location, resulting in a great deal of redundant customization (because the same customization, or at least very similar customizations, must be performed in a decentralized fashion at implementing companies). In case the point is elusive, this is exactly what has happened with ERP systems.

An alternate development approach is to decompose the transaction to its behavior per dimension, provide an initial set of common dimension combinations, and allow the transaction to be easily extended. This can happen by simply copying over a pre-existing transaction variant and making a single change to a dimension behavior (or to multiple dimension behaviors), resulting in a new transaction variant. An example of this is shown below:

Transaction Dimensions

Transaction Identifier	"Business" Name	Send from Location	Send to Location	Invoice from Location	Invoice to Location
A1	Non Billing Stock Tranport Order	A	B	None	None
A2	Standard Billing Stock Tranport Order	A	B	B	A
A3	Asychronous Billing Stock Tranport Order Version 1	A	B	C	A
A4	Asychronous Billing Stock Tranport Order Version 2	A	B	D	A
A5	etc				

The total library of the transactions categories and variants within those categories constitutes the total of the functionality within any ERP system.

What I have described above would be the perfect scenario, but ERP systems were not designed this way. And because of their transactional inflexibility, the tight integration of their modules means that they restrict the ability of companies to fully leverage the functionalities in applications that are connected to ERP systems. Thus a company with an ERP system will receive less value from any other application that they implement (unless the application is extremely simple) than a company that does not have an ERP system. This is one of the major reasons why most ERP systems are either a dead end—or simply a starter kit setting a company for much more expense and work down the road.

Conclusion

This chapter described several areas where ERP hampers the ability of companies to find the best functionality for their needs. For example, ERP systems set a low standard for BOM management, but this standard has since become accepted as how things are done. Because the BOM cannot be effectively managed in ERP, and because most companies do not buy BOM management software, Excel is used to manage BOMs. The limitations in using spreadsheets to create and manage BOMs have been extensively documented in my book, *The Bill of Materials in Excel, Planning, ERP and PLM/BMMS Software* and at Arena Solutions' website.

Collaboration is a second example of a dead end created by ERP systems. Companies are severely restricted in their ability to collaborate with suppliers and customers because they over rely on ERP. Any collaboration that does occur must take place through another application that is connected to the ERP system. Amazingly, after all these years, the majority of collaboration between companies is managed by either EDI or simple flat file transfers by e-mail or to FTP accounts. It should be noted that not all ERP systems offer such limited functionality. Rootstock, which provides three of the four modules, does not limit companies in this way. But the largest and most frequently installed ERP systems (Tier 1 and Tier 2 categories) do. This chapter finished off with one example of how ERP undermines internal/external planning arrangements, and also an example of intercompany transfers.

These were just four examples, but in reality the examples go on and on. When it comes to functionality, ERP offers mediocrity. After working with mediocre functionality for many years, companies become accepting of mediocre solutions, meaning that they are saddled with lagging functionality. They come to the conclusion that the functionality in ERP is "good enough" and that ERP is the best way to perform activities. But why is that perception considered accurate? For instance, it is well known that ERP does not do collaboration.

Many companies think they can manage the BOM with ERP. While ERP systems do have the ability to hold BOMs; they just can't originate or manage BOMs. However, companies paid quite a lot of money for the bad BOM functionality that they do have—significantly more than if they had purchased a best-of-breed solution—and they have little choice but to stay the course. As a result, they are unable to gain the efficiency of sharing the BOM with both internal users and external users. Why is that considered good enough?

These were just a few examples of the pervasive issue that affects decisions of how to access software functionality in companies that have implemented ERP systems—there is a constant pressure to use the ERP system's functionality, when this is not the best or even competitive functionality when one compares it with what is available outside of the ERP system.

CHAPTER 11

Alternatives to ERP or Adjusting the Current ERP System

ERP promoters make a serious misrepresentation in their discussions of ERP by suggesting that there is **no alternative** to ERP. To think that there is no alternative, one would have to be biased (either financially—they work in or somehow make money from ERP—or non-financially—they are simply used to ERP environments), or they simply don't understand the enterprise software market very well. Actually there are plenty of alternatives to ERP. Some of the alternatives call themselves "ERP" because this has **become** desired terminology, even though they would not meet the technical definition of ERP.

Is Criticism of ERP Simply Negative and Counterproductive?

As part of a broader and quite interesting article about enterprise software, Cynthia Rettig was critical of ERP and SOA software and implementations. In this article, she begins with the following explanation of how IT grew as a percentage of investment since 1970.

> *"Back-office systems—including both software applications and the data they process—are a variegated patchwork of*

systems, containing fifty or more databases and hundreds of separate software programs installed over decades and interconnected by idiosyncratic, Byzantine and poorly documented customized processes. To manage this growing complexity, IT departments have grown substantially: As a percentage of total investment, IT rose from 2.6 percent to 3.5 percent between 1970 and 1980. By 1990 IT consumed 9 percent, and by 1999 a whopping 22 percent of total investment went to IT. Growth in IT spending has fallen off, but it is nonetheless surprising to hear that today's IT departments spend 70 percent to 80 percent of their budgets just trying to keep existing systems running.

"But these massive programs, with millions of lines of code, thousands of installation options and countless interrelated pieces, introduced new levels of complexity, often without eliminating the older systems (known as 'legacy' systems) they were designed to replace. In addition, concurrent technological and business changes made closed ERP systems organized around products less than a perfect solution: Just as companies were undertaking multiyear ERP implementations, the Internet was evolving into a major new force, changing the way companies transacted business with their customers, suppliers and partners. At the same time, businesses were realizing that organizing their information around customers and services—and using newly available customer relationship management systems—was critical to their success.

"The concept of a single monolithic system failed for many companies. Different divisions or facilities often made independent purchases, and other systems were inherited through mergers and acquisitions. Thus, many companies ended up having several instances of the same ERP systems or a variety of different ERP systems altogether, further complicating their IT landscape. In the end, ERP systems became just another subset of the legacy systems they were supposed to replace."

So much money now flows from the ERP industry that criticism is not well tolerated. A lot of water has passed under the bridge here; many entities (whose pockets would be lined by the sale) recommended ERP systems to clients, even though there was no evidence that the ERP systems would improve the condition of these companies. Several of those who criticized Cynthia Rettig had the following to say:

> *"There's really nothing new in [Ms. Rettig's] analysis. But Rettig goes a step further and says there's no hope for the future. In fact, while she doesn't offer any remedies for her gloomy prognosis, she does quash one—service-oriented architecture (SOA)."*

The beginning of this quotation provides an example of the logical fallacy argument from repetition. Those who dislike research or someone else's conclusions, but do not have anything of substance to add offer this standard criticism. Rettig disagrees with the proposal that SOA will solve the problems of ERP (a prognosis that ended up being true). Why is that considered *"gloomy"*? If there is little evidence that SOA will remedy the issues with ERP, then why invest resources into it?

Secondly, if there is *"nothing new"* in Rettig's analysis, perhaps the analysis is synthesized in a different way. Furthermore, I read through countless articles on ERP that repeated unfounded statements regarding the benefits of ERP—and Rettig's analysis, and I can't recall anyone criticizing these generic articles that could have come off of a copy machine from previous articles, yet one of the first articles to be critical of ERP as a concept is not new? What is this author's definition of new?

The explanation that ERP systems have performed poorly by any measure and have a bleak future is not generally accepted, so her analysis is new in the sense that it explains something that is generally not known. Actually Rettig's article is novel in many ways; it is not original research, but does a nice job referencing multiple sources of original research. Furthermore, there is nothing new in the multitude of articles about the opportunity of ERP or about getting more value from ERP, or how SOA was going to make all the ERP investments worthwhile. But no one seems to criticize those articles—because they are **promotional**.

In terms of the criticism regarding *"not offering any remedies,"* firstly, not every form of analysis needs to provide a solution. The very idea that research or observations need to provide remedies (why would anyone think that is true?), is itself a pretext for rejecting research. This does not provide a positive outlook. In fact, the remedy should be self-evident: reduce one's investment in ERP software, and do not place one's bet on SOA as a solution. As it turns out, this remedy would have been the correct choice.

This type of criticism deliberately evades the obvious behavioral adjustment that is implicit with Cynthia Rettig's analysis. As long as the standard is what is positive rather than what is true, the evidence required for a promotional statement will always be lower than the evidence required for a critical statement.

Reducing ERP Dependency

Companies will benefit if they reduce their dependency on ERP—particularly "Big ERP"—in even small ways. Any redirection of resources away from ERP (for example, replacing ERP functionality with external systems) should benefit the company over the long term. However, companies that buy new non-ERP software that helps them manage their businesses better rather than their ERP software must still pay the support cost of the system, and they will pay the same amount even if they turn off portions of their ERP system. This is a major reason as to why so many companies have continued to implement uncompetitive functionality in their ERP systems when so many better solutions are available in the marketplace: they are attempting to utilize their pre-existing investment in their ERP system.

However, research at our companion site Software Decisions demonstrates that this is a faulty logic: companies can only expect to save 12.5 percent of the application's TCO by leveraging the sunk cost of a previously implemented ERP system.[62] Other applications that are specifically designed to meet business requirements (aka best-of-breed) have better ratings in a variety of compensating criteria. Companies must consider which costs are higher: the cost to purchase better software plus pay the support cost of their ERP system, or the continuing indirect costs associated with their ERP system, including:

1. A longer implementation

2. More customization expense

---

[62] This website can be viewed at http://www.softwaredecisions.org.

3. A higher-risk implementation

4. Lower functionality/worse fit of functionality

5. Lower usability

6. Lower maintainability

The Research is Conclusive for the Negative Hypothesis

Once all the negatives are recognized, ERP cannot even be shown to improve the financial performance of companies. The only real demonstrated benefit of ERP has been to the **ERP vendors and to implementation companies**, not to the actual buyers of ERP software. A purchase of an ERP system is an extremely effective way to lock in a customer to a vendor, and to allow the vendor to sell other applications to current customers. Have ERP systems been beneficial for SAP, Oracle, IBM, Deloitte and all manner of consulting companies? There the evidence is clear: ERP has greatly benefited those that sell and implement ERP software. Therefore, if you want to benefit from ERP, sell it or implement it, but don't buy it.

ERP Adjustment

The value of Big ERP is just not there. Some of the highest rates in the enterprise software space are being charged for what amounts to basic functionality. The resources can be transitioned from Big ERP to applications that offer a better ROI.

ERP disintegration is a term that I have coined to describe what should be the next phase of ERP: that is, to begin to give up the long-dead idea that ERP can meet all of a company's needs (the original proposition for ERP), and that "getting the most" out of ERP is the best strategy for a company to follow. Getting the most from ERP translates very simply to giving the least to your business. Rather than trying to get ERP to do things that it is not good at doing, more diverse applications should be brought into the fold, along with more analytical skills. The ERP period was a period when many people turned their brains off and put their trust in ERP vendors and in official "authorities" (all of whom had financial conflicts of interest) to answer all of their question and to meet all of their requirements. With ERP disintegration, true system integration skills will be brought back within implementing companies and custom solutions will be developed that fit the company's needs.

On average, companies still have 60 percent of their ERP systems modules implemented. It's been a long road and the payoff has been poor. It is now all too obvious that the promise of ERP will not be realized, and it will not get better in the future. Too often, applications were purchased from the ERP vendors because customers preferred to go with familiar vendors over vendors whose software best met their business requirements. IT departments have been covering up the deficiencies in software purchased from the major ERP vendors for many years now, and it has led to poor outcomes. Companies looking for the easiest route to enhancing the value of their IT spend should break the cycle of dependency on their ERP vendors and create a competitive environment that rewards software innovation and the best software available. This means running tighter and more analytical software selections, and comparing what is currently implemented in the ERP system against applications that could improve the area.[63]

Free from Overinvestment in ERP

Freed from overinvestment in ERP, the company is able to choose the best software for its needs in each area and then integrate this software directly to the finance system. However, for those who already have ERP, the question becomes: What to do with the ERP system, and how to best leverage it?

Essentially, the effect of the ERP system must be minimized. Different areas of the ERP system will gradually cede ground to other applications and the more quickly this happens, the more quickly companies can improve their IT by leveraging the better functionality in non-ERP applications. As a result, ERP vendors will have less influence over your company, and your company may not need to upgrade its ERP system as frequently. Remember that there is no reason to look to other software from the ERP vendors, or to give their software preferential treatment.

One approach to detaching from your ERP system is to deactivate complete modules or portions of modules. ERP systems are modular, and in fact, most companies

---

[63] The analytical tools to do this are provided in the SCM Focus Press book, *Enterprise Software Selection: How to Pinpoint the Perfect Software Solution using Multiple Information Sources.*

have not implemented all of the modules in their ERP system, but instead continue to use other applications and connect them to the ERP system—although they pay a high price in integration costs and functionality incompatibility to do so. A company can run one module or several modules, and can slowly decommission portions of each module and attach best-of-breed applications. A company that is running a sales and distribution module, along with a production planning module and finance/accounting module, could deactivate the production planning module and instead use a best-of-breed production planning and execution system from the vendor of their choice. They would then integrate this production planning module back to the ERP sales module and the finance/accounting module, instead of integrating the external production planning and execution system to the production planning module, which would then interact with the sales module and the finance/accounting module.

Replacement of Part of ERP

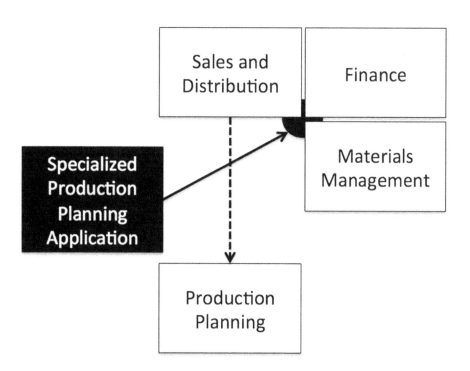

There are plenty of alternatives to an ERP centric approach, and many companies use them. I have included a few alternatives in this book, but this book is really directed toward a review of the research on ERP. The book, *Replacing Big ERP: Breaking the Big ERP Habit with Best of Breed Applications at a Fraction of the Cost* is where I focus on alternatives and where I compare a best-of-breed strategy against a 100 percent ERP and ERP vendor solution.

ERP Alternatives Per Company Size

Larger companies tend to be the bread and butter of large ERP vendors such as SAP and Oracle. Mid-sized companies do not use anywhere near the amount of functionality offered by these software vendors. SAP and Oracle started off building their software around the needs of big companies. They adjusted their software to appeal to smaller companies, but their solutions are simply overkill for anything but the larger companies.[64]

Therefore, when people address the topic of Big ERP, it is from the perspective that ERP has proven something—at least at big companies. When they do this, they essentially accept the assumptions they have heard from the marketing departments of ERP vendors and their lieutenants, the large consulting companies. As I have shown in this book, research has proven that the fanciful projections regarding ERP were simply marketing hyperbole. To accept the position that "ERP must be helpful" is to accept something that has never been proven. It is *argumentum ad numerum*—a fallacious argument—that concludes the proposal is true because many people (and companies) believe it to be true.

Conclusion

Executive decision-makers undermine their software selection process when they attempt to validate the statements about and capabilities of applications that neither they, nor other people in their company, have experience with. The executive decision-maker is in a position of weakness, which makes it difficult for them to make informed decisions. First-hand experience regarding all enterprise software is available and can be found on LinkedIn or Dice. Independent consultants may be hired full-time and work on-site, or be hired remotely, depending upon the

---

[64] SAP discontinued their development of SAP Business ByDesign, an attempt to develop a solution for mid-sized companies.

circumstances and the consultant's availability. An independent consultant is far more reliable than a consulting company for advising on a software selection. Unlike a major consulting firm, an independent consultant is not attempting to staff consultants on the project. However, in order to minimize bias, it should be explained to the independent consultant that they will not be part of the implementation in any way. This removes any potential for financial bias and makes the consultant indifferent as to which software the company decides to implement.

CHAPTER 12

Conclusion

Economics gave us the useful term of "externality." When an entity engages in a behavior that places costs on other entities for which it does not compensate them, this is referred to as a **negative** externality. The ERP craze has been primarily an exercise in the perpetuation of a negative externality on the part of ERP vendors and ERP implementation companies on ERP buyers, and given the evidence of poor ERP functionality and costs, it is amazing that it has gone on for this long. It is the greatest misallocation of resources in the still relatively young enterprise software industry.

My analysis of the research into ERP systems tells a very interesting story about how software is purchased. I have explained the issue of ERP systems to a number of people—from executives to technical resources, to laypeople. A very effective analogy to use with people not familiar with ERP is to think of ERP as an octopus. ERP systems began as one thing, and now they are an unruly and expensive octopus, which connects throughout the enterprise but mostly in unproductive ways. The following quotation brings up an interesting point that more companies should consider.

"Over the last two decades, companies have plowed many billions of dollars into enterprise resource planning (ERP) systems and the hardware required to run them. But what, in the long run, will be the legacy of ERP? Will it be viewed as it has been promoted by its marketers: as a milestone in business automation that allowed companies to integrate their previously fragmented information systems and simplify their data flows? Or will it be viewed as a stopgap that largely backfired by tangling companies in even more systems complexity and even higher IT costs?" — Nicolas Carr

ERP software is a category of software with a very low ROI (if one limits the financial returns to the ERP system itself), and a negative ROI when one looks at how ERP negatively impacts a company's overall software investment—for instance, the negative affect on the company's other applications, as well as how ERP isolates companies from customers and suppliers.

In the SCM Focus Press book, *Enterprise Software Selection: How to Pinpoint the Perfect Software Solution using Multiple Information Sources,* I describe how most companies that buy enterprise software lack the internal ability **to validate the claims** made by software vendors. In addition, they are often led down the garden path to a bad decision by consulting companies that place their interests ahead of their clients. ERP systems became so popular because the actual claims about their benefits were **never** analyzed properly. Because ERP systems have been so lucrative for software vendors and consulting companies, there has been a strong incentive for them to get companies to purchase them. For decades, when a company complained to their consultants about their current system's shortcomings, the consultants commonly responded that what the company really needed was an ERP system (cue the oversimplified explanation of how ERP systems integrate all of the company's processes). One can imagine how many times this same conversation has played itself out at companies around the globe. The unfortunate fact of the matter is that most ERP systems were purchased without appropriate research; a very large percentage of them were purchased because they were seen as the "thing" to implement. This faulty logic controls many IT purchase decisions, as the following quotation attests.

"Interviews with the managers confirmed that if a successful strategic IT (e.g., laptops to salespeople) was implemented by one or two firms, the other competitors soon followed the lead. Thus, although the IT intensity of the industry increased, no net performance effect was observed." — The Relationship Between Investment in Information Technology and Firm Performance: A Study of the Valve Manufacturing Sector, Information Systems Research

At its heart, ERP was a misleading and oversimplified, although a highly compelling, concept. It was never a good investment and now hinders a company's ability to leverage the Internet and **reduces its ability** to gain value from its other applications.

ERP was based upon several false assumptions that have been explained throughout this book. The central premise of ERP—that you could have a single set of integration applications from a single vendor that would always meet the implementing company's needs and therefore greatly reduce and almost eliminate the need to integrate to other applications—was delusional when it was first proposed and is even more delusional now. The development of information systems in the form of Internet and SaaS solutions has worked in the opposite direction of ERP. The future of information systems will involve mixing and matching the best solutions from a variety of vendors, with much of the data storage and processing being handled remotely. The IT burden on companies will be greatly reduced, and ERP has no place in this model. The more that companies cling to their ERP investments, the less they will be able to participate in this open approach to accessing application functionality. Forward-thinking companies will consider their ERP investments as what they are: sunk costs. They will migrate to better functionality in other systems and take a piecemeal approach to ERP.

The logics that were used to sell ERP systems was never anything more than hypotheses. When I explain why any well-promoted concept should have evidence to support it, often the listener simply repeats the hypothesis back to me. At that point, I have to say, *"Yes that is the hypothesis, but there is no evidence to support it."* Of course, anyone has the right to propose any hypothesis they like. However, while a hypothesis may turn out to "make sense" or seem likely, it's only through testing that we can know for sure. If a hypothesis has had a full opportunity to be tested (after 30 years, ERP has certainly had this opportunity) and has proven false, then it is time to dispense with the hypothesis and to move to a new one. That is how all knowledge advances.

Two powerful vendors—SAP and Oracle—were installed at the top of the enterprise software hierarchy because of ERP. This development has been bad for the enterprise software market, as these two actors have abused their power by offering their clients low value and high costs, and by using account control techniques. Many other ERP vendors were never able to capitalize on their ability to sell ERP software and to sell other types of software.

Is There Truly No Alternative to ERP?
Proponents of ERP make it sound as if there are no alternatives to ERP, or that the alternatives are "poorly integrated" (which is another way of saying that there are no alternatives). A misleading argumentative technique frequently used by people who are not interested in evaluating or discussing alternatives is to judge ideas as not representing valid alternatives. When an alternative is presented, they may say, *"That is not a real alternative,"* when it is in fact an alternative; it is simply not an alternative they agree with. Arguments are certainly simplified when you state that all other alternatives are not real alternatives, do not provide evidence to support your claims, and announce that you have chosen the one true alternative. The following quotation is an example of this type of argument.

> *"If I'm a major enterprise, especially a manufacturer, what's the cost of NOT having an ERP system?"*

This frames the question in the reverse and is an example of the logical fallacy of shifting the burden of proof. It is designed to essentially ask the person on the other side of the argument to prove that ERP is not a good investment. This is called "proving a negative." The responder is asked to prove that ERP is not a good investment. This is not how proof works in science. We don't start off by making a contention, providing no evidence, and then asking the other person to prove our statement is incorrect. But since the question was asked...the bulk of evidence shows that the benefits of ERP systems are small. Therefore, naturally, the costs of **not** having an ERP system are less than the cost of **having** an ERP system, both in terms of implicit and explicit costs. A company with no ERP system will incur fewer software-related costs and gain better functionality (by choosing the best software for its needs rather than whatever their ERP vendor is offering).

> *"What are my alternatives to accomplish the same objectives? I submit those alternatives are few and poorly integrated."*

There are a wide variety of alternatives available to accomplish the same objectives. Quite a few financial and accounting applications can be selected and connected to any number of other applications in order to replicate (and greatly exceed) what ERP does. The alternatives are not "few"—they are many. These alternatives are presented in the SCM Focus Press book, *Replacing ERP: Breaking the ERP Habit with Flexible Applications at a Fraction of the Cost.*

Secondly, while ERP systems are better integrated to **themselves**, which is a highly parochial way of looking at integration, ERP offers **no** integration benefit for connecting to a company's other systems, and may offer higher integration costs than non-ERP environments. Here is a further quotation from the failed Air Force's ECSS initiative:

> *"It's not worth the money to poorly implement anything. It's worth the money to take the time, hire people with the appropriate knowledge, and do the necessary planning and testing to minimize the chances of an ERP installation failing."*

In this statement, the individuals take the common approach to analyzing ERP failures: the failure of the ERP project was related 100 percent to how it was implemented and not related to issues with the ERP system itself. How do faulty implementation methodologies explain the low satisfaction rate with ERP systems as a whole? How did a system, which has never shown much financial and operational benefit to companies, gain its halo? Were all ERP systems incorrectly implemented? These types of comments are extremely common among ERP proponents, but they offer no evidence and no new information. They provide nothing more than an excuse, which—thirty years into ERP history—is becoming somewhat stale.

The evidence, which few have any interest in reviewing, is that ERP systems produce a meager return on investment, and in other ways are major distractions for companies, drawing energy away from other initiatives. All of the investment of time and money in ERP must be compared against what it could provide if invested in other areas.

MRP and the History of MRP

If computers had been developed several hundred years earlier, it is very likely that MRP would have followed the development of computing shortly thereafter. In fact, MRP was developed around 1961, but did not become broadly implemented in software until around 1975—which, not coincidentally, is the beginnings of the commercial software industry—although as a method it is thought that **MRP** was practiced in at least a simple form prior to the 1940s in Europe.[65]

---

[65] MRP Contributes to a Company's Profitability.

MRP is one of the major historical methods that performs a variety of functions from inventory management to production planning.

Prior to 1970, a term that we use so commonly today—software—was essentially unused. One of the earliest systems to be used by business was the IBM system developed for American Airlines called SABRE (Semi Automated Business Research Environment), which had its first incarnation in 1960 in what was the first commercial application of its type. SABRE was developed based upon a military program called SAGE (Semi Automated Ground Environment), which was designed to monitor Soviet bombers. And at that time, most of the programming and software development work was for military purposes, and the extremely fast uptake of these types of systems was surprising to many who worked in the industry at this time.[66]

Other Books from SCM Focus

Bill of Materials in Excel, ERP, Planning and PLM/BMMS Software

http://www.scmfocus.com/scmfocuspress/the-software-approaches-for-improving-your-bill-of-materials-book/

Constrained Supply and Production Planning with SAP APO

http://www.scmfocus.com/scmfocuspress/select-a-book/constrained-supply-and-production-planning-in-sap-apo/

---

[66] Determining when the software industry was "created" is difficult because it depends upon what one means by "software." Software goes back to the first electronic computers in the 1940s, but these were highly expensive and rare applications for things like code breaking. Not only were these applications not generally known, but were classified. We only know about them now because this information has been declassified by the US and the UK.

One limitation to the use of software was the available hardware: *"In the 1960s, computer memory and mass storage were scarce and expensive. Early core memory cost one dollar per bit. Popular commercial computers, such as the IBM 1401, shipped with as little as 2 Kbytes of memory. Programs often mimicked card-processing techniques."* — Wikipedia. It's difficult to do very much when one has so little ability to process the software.

Actually, a second issue was coding efficiency. Early computers were programmed in machine and assembly language, which was quite inefficient. COBOL, the first higher-level programming language for business, was not introduced until 1959. Of course it took time for individuals to build their skills developing software with this language.

A third issue was the regulatory environment, which caused IBM to unbundle hardware from software.

Enterprise Software Risk: Controlling the Main Risk Factors on IT Projects

http://www.scmfocus.com/scmfocuspress/it-decision-making-books/enterprise-software-project-risk-management/

Enterprise Software Selection: How to Pinpoint the Perfect Software Solution using Multiple Information Sources

http://www.scmfocus.com/scmfocuspress/it-decision-making-books/enterprise-software-selection/

Enterprise Software TCO: Calculating and Using Total Cost of Ownership for Decision Making

http://www.scmfocus.com/scmfocuspress/it-decision-making-books/enterprise-software-tco/

Gartner and the Magic Quadrant: A Guide for Buyers, Vendors, Investors

http://www.scmfocus.com/scmfocuspress/it-decision-making-books/gartner-and-the-magic-quadrant/

Inventory Optimization and Multi-Echelon Planning Software

http://www.scmfocus.com/scmfocuspress/supply-books/the-inventory-optimization-and-multi-echelon-software-book/

Multi Method Supply Planning in SAP APO

http://www.scmfocus.com/scmfocuspress/select-a-book/multi-method-supply-planning-in-sap-apo/

Planning Horizons, Calendars and Timings in SAP APO

http://www.scmfocus.com/scmfocuspress/select-a-book/planning-horizons-calendars-and-timings-in-sap-apo/

Process Industry Manufacturing Software: ERP, Planning, Recipe, MES & Process Control

http://www.scmfocus.com/scmfocuspress/production-books/process-industry-planning/

Replacing Big ERP: Breaking the Big ERP Habit with Best of Breed Applications at a Fraction of the Cost

http://www.scmfocus.com/scmfocuspress/erp-books/replacing-erp/

Setting Up the Supply Network in SAP APO

http://www.scmfocus.com/scmfocuspress/select-a-book/setting-up-the-supply-network-in-sap-apo/

SuperPlant: Creating a Nimble Manufacturing Enterprise with Adaptive Planning

http://www.scmfocus.com/scmfocuspress/production-books/the-superplant-concept/

Supply Chain Forecasting Software

http://www.scmfocus.com/scmfocuspress/the-statistical-and-consensus-supply-chain-forecasting-software-book/

Supply Planning with MRP, DRP and APS Software

http://www.scmfocus.com/scmfocuspress/supply-books/the-supply-planning-with-mrpdrp-and-aps-software-book/

Spreading the Word

SCM Focus Press is a small publisher. However, we pride ourselves on publishing the unvarnished truth that most other publishers will not publish. If you felt like you learned something valuable from reading this book, please spread the word by adding a review to our page on Amazon.com.

Software Decisions

This site offers a variety of cost and risk comparisons between Big ERP, Tier 2 ERP and a 100 percent best-of-breed solution. You can find out more about the estimators at our Software Decisions website.

http://www.softwaredecisions.org

Author Profile

Shaun Snapp is the Founder and Editor of SCM Focus. SCM Focus is one of the largest independent supply chain software analysis and educational sites on the Internet.

After working at several of the largest consulting companies and at i2 Technologies, he became an independent consultant and later started SCM Focus. He maintains a strong interest in comparative software design, and works both in SAP APO, as well as with a variety of best-of-breed supply chain planning vendors. His ongoing relationships with these vendors keep him on the cutting edge of emerging technology.

Primary Sources of Information and Writing Topics

Shaun writes about topics with which he has first-hand experience. These topics range from recovering problematic implementations, to system configuration, to socializing complex software and supply chain concepts in the areas of demand planning, supply planning and production planning.

More broadly, he writes on topics supportive of these applications, which include master data parameter management, integration, analytics, simulation and bill of material management systems. He covers management aspects of enterprise software ranging from software policy to handling consulting partners on SAP projects.

Shaun writes from an implementer's perspective and as a result he focuses on how software is actually used in practice rather than its hypothetical or "pure release note capabilities." Unlike many authors in enterprise software who keep their distance from discussing the realities of software implementation, he writes both on the problems as well as the successes of his software use. This gives him a distinctive voice in the field.

Secondary Sources of Information

In addition to project experience, Shaun's interest in academic literature is a secondary source of information for his books and articles. Intrigued with the historical perspective of supply chain software, much of his writing is influenced by his readings and research into how different categories of supply chain software developed, evolved, and finally became broadly used over time.

Covering the Latest Software Developments

Shaun is focused on supply chain software selections and implementation improvement through writing and consulting, bringing companies some of the newest technologies and methods. Some of the software developments that Shaun showcases at SCM Focus and in books at SCM Focus Press have yet to reach widespread adoption.

Education

Shaun has an undergraduate degree in business from the University of Hawaii, a Masters of Science in Maritime Management from the Maine Maritime Academy and a Masters of Science in Business Logistics from Penn State University. He has taught both logistics and SAP software.

Software Certifications

Shaun has been trained and/or certified in applications from i2 Technologies, Servigistics, ToolsGroup and SAP (SD, DP, SNP, SPP, EWM).

Contact

Shaun can be contacted at: shaunsnapp@scmfocus.com www.scmfocus.com/

Vendor Acknowledgements and Profiles

Below are brief profiles of each vendor for which screen shots have been included in this book.

Arena Solutions

Arena is the leading SaaS-based PLM/bill of material management software vendor in the world. Arena is a low-cost provider and leader in the areas of security, collaboration, and the management of a multi-tenant system, which can be accessed by people around the world.

www.arenasolutions.com

ERPNext (Web Notes Technologies)

Web Notes Technologies is an Internet engineering company based out of Mumbai founded in 2008. They build web based Open Source applications for everyone to use. ERPNext is their flagship product and is used by hundreds of users worldwide. Web Notes Technologies has won numerous open source awards.

http://www.erpnext.com

Rootstock

Launched in 2008, Rootstock Software is a proven provider of powerful Cloud ERP manufacturing, distribution and supply chain solutions that enable manufacturers and distributors to cut costs, improve processes, and increase revenue with minimal IT infrastructure investment. The company has grown to serve customers throughout North America, Europe and Asia Pacific and is now available exclusively on the salesforce.com's Salesforce Platform (Force.com) and available through the saleforce.com AppExchange, the world's most-popular marketplace for business apps.

http://www.rootstock.com

SAP

SAP does not need much of an introduction. They are the largest vendor of enterprise software applications for supply chain management. SAP has multiple applications that are showcased in this book, including SAP ERP and SAP SCM/APO SNP and SAP SCM/APO SPP.

www.sap.com

Links in the Book

Chapter 1

http://www.scmfocus.com/writing-rules/

http://www.scmfocus.com/

http://www.scmfocus.com/scmfocuspress/it-decision-making-books/
the-real-story-behind-erp/

Chapter 2

http://www.scmfocus.com/scmhistory/2012/08/the-history-of-mrp-
and-drp/

Chapter 5

http://www.scmfocus.com/sapplanning/2011/05/19/why-i-no-longer-
recommend-using-the-cif/

http://www.scmfocus.com/sapplanning/2012/10/30/the-cif-
administrator/

http://www.scmfocus.com/sapintegration/2011/11/15/what-are-saps-
vendor-integration-certifications-worth-on-projects/

http://www.scmfocus.com/enterprisesoftwarepolicy/2011/11/16/
everyone-in-enterprise-software-is-afraid-of-the-big-sap-bully/

Chapter 6

http://www.scmfocus.com/inventoryoptimizationmultiechelon/2010/01/its-time-for-the-sap-xapps-program-to-die/

http://www.scmfocus.com/enterprisesoftwarepolicy/2012/01/27/how-common-is-it-for-sap-to-take-intellectual-property-from-partners/

http://help.sap.com/saphelp_SCM700_ehp01/helpdata/en/48/aae32a8740356ce
10000000a421937/frameset.htm

http://www.scmfocus.com/sapprojectmanagement/2010/07/sap-will-never-support-soa/

Chapter 7

http://www.softwaredecisions.org

Chapter 8

http://www.scmfocus.com/enterprisesoftwarepolicy/2013/11/09/fiduciary-liability-it-consulting-companies-have-no-fiduciary-duty/

http://www.scmfocus.com/sapprojectmanagement/2013/08/maximum-tolerable-functionality/

http://www.scmfocus.com/supplyplanning/2011/07/09/what-is-your-supply-planning-optimizer-optimizing/

http://www.scmfocus.com/inventoryoptimizationmultiechelon/2011/05/how-costs-are-really-set-in-cost-optimization-implementations/

Chapter 10

http://www.scmfocus.com/supplychaincollaboration/2010/06/where-are-the-supply-chain-collaboration-success-stories/

http://www.scmfocus.com/supplychaincollaboration/2013/07/
why-must-specialized-supply-chain-collaboration-applications-exist/

http://www.scmfocus.com/scmhistory/2013/08/earliest-edi/

http://www.scmfocus.com/erp/2013/10/20/does-a-company-that-performs-no-manufacturing-and-no-distribution-require-an-erp-system/

Chapter 11

http://www.softwaredecisions.org

Abbreviations

API: Application Program Interface

BOM: Bill of Materials

CAD: Computer Aided Design

CAM: Computer Aided Manufacturing

CM: Contract Manufacturer

CRM: Customer Relationship Management

DRP: Distribution Resource Planning

ECSS: Expeditionary Combat Support System

EDI: Electronic Data Interchange

ERP: Enterprise Resource Planning

MES: Manufacturing Execution Scheduling

MRP: Material Requirements Planning

MRP II: Manufacturing Resource Planning

OEM: Original Equipment Manufacturer

PLM: Product Life Cycle Management

ROA: Return on Assets

ROI: Return on Investment

ROS: Return on Sales

SaaS: Software as a Service

SABRE: Semi Automated Business Research Environment

SAGE: Semi Automated Ground Environment

SCM: Supply Chain Management

SOA: Service Oriented Architecture

STO: Stock Transfer Order

STR: Stock Transport Requisition

TCO: Total Cost of Ownership

Y2K: Year 2000

QMS: Quality Management Systems

References

Aghazadeh, Seyed-Mahmoud. *MRP Contributes to a Company's Profitability*. 2003.

Al-Mashari, Majed. Al-Mudimigh, Abdulla. Ziari, Mohamed. *Enterprise Resource Planning: A Taxonomy of Critical Factors*. European Journal of Operations Research, June 2002.

Angell, Marcia. *The Truth About the Drug Companies*. July 15, 2004. http://www.wanttoknow.info/truthaboutdrugcompanies.

Antidepressant Medications Are Ineffective and Misleading. http://truthindrugs.com/pdf/ads.pdf.

Baase, Sara. *IBM: Producer or Predator*. April 1974. http://www-rohan.sdsu.edu/faculty/giftfire/ibm.html.

Bardach, Eugene. *A Practical Guide for Policy Analysis: The Eightfold Path to More Effective Problem Solving (4th Edition)*. CQ Press: College Publishing Group, 2011.

Bartholomew, Doug. *Realizing ERP's Untapped Potential. Pharmaceutical Manufacturing*. September 7, 2005. http://www.pharmamanufacturing.com/articles/2004/242/.

Bezruchka, Stephen. *The Hurrider I Go, The Behinder I Get: The Deteriorating International Ranking of U.S. Health Status*. January 3, 2012. http://www.annualreviews.org/doi/pdf/10.1146/annurev-publhealth-031811-124649.

Biello, David. *Grass Makes Better Ethanol than Corn Does.* Scientific American. January 8, 2008. http://www.scientificamerican.com/article.cfm?id=grass-makes-better-ethanol-than-corn.

Birch, Nicholas. *Why ERP Doesn't Work.* June 2007. http://www.istart.co.nz/index/HM20/PC0/PVC197/EX27129/AR29697.

Bridgwater, Adrian. *ERP is Dead, Long Live Two-Tier ERP.* December 12, 2012. http://www.computerweekly.com/blogs/cwdn/2012/12/erp-is-dead-long-live-two-tier-erp.html.

Burns, Michael. *What Does an ERP System Cost?* CA Magazine. August 2011. http://www.camagazine.com/archives/print-edition/2011/aug/columns/camagazine50480.aspx.

Castenllina, Nick. *To ERP or Not to ERP: In Manufacturing, It Isn't Even a Question.* March 31, 2011. http://aberdeen.com/aberdeen-library/7116/RA-enterprise-resource-planning.aspx.

Chen, Injazz J. *Planning for ERP Systems: Analysis and Future Trend.* Business Process Management Journal, 2001. Chiappinelli, Chris. *New ERP Paradigm Challenges Old Assumptions.* March 2, 2011. www.techmatchpro.com/article/2011/3/new-erp-paradigm-challenges-old-assumptions.

Clarke, Gavin. *Larry 'Shared Databases are Crap' Ellison Reveals Shared Oracle Database.* October 1, 2012. http://www.theregister.co.uk/2012/10/01/ellison_oow_2012_database_cloud/.

Columbus, Louis. *ERP Prediction for 2013: The Customer Takes Control.* Forbes, January 7, 2013. http://www.forbes.com/sites/louiscolumbus/2013/01/07/erp-prediction-for-2013-the-customer-takes-control/.

Corn Ethanol. Accessed July 3, 2013. http://en.wikipedia.org/wiki/Corn_ethanol.

Elragal, Ahmed and Al-Serafi, Ayman. *The Effect of ERP System Implementation on Business Performance: An Exploratory Case-Study.* June 2011. http://www.ibimapublishing.com/journals/CIBIMA/2011/670212/670212.pdf.

Enterprise Resource Planning. Accessed July 23, 2013. http://en.wikipedia.org/wiki/Enterprise_resource_planning.

ERP: Is High ROI with Low TCO Possible? Aberdeen Group, 2012.

Fear, Uncertainty and Doubt. Accessed August 25, 2013.
   http://en.wikipedia.org/wiki/Fear,_uncertainty_and_doubt.

Hall, Susan. *Third-Party ERP Support: When It Makes Sense.* October 4, 2012.
   http://www.enterpriseappstoday.com/erp/third-party-erp-support-when-it-makes-sense.html.

Hawthorne Effect. Accessed July 16, 2013.
   http://en.wikipedia.org/wiki/Hawthorne_effect.

Henry Ford. Last modified November 6, 2013.
   http://en.wikipedia.org/wiki/Henry_Ford.

History of IBM. Accessed July 26, 2013.
   http://en.wikipedia.org/wiki/History_of_IBM.

Insel, Thomas. *Directors Blog: Antidepressants: A Complicated Picture.* December 6, 2011.
   http://www.nimh.nih.gov/about/director/2011/antidepressants-a-complicated-picture.shtml.

Jurtras, Mint. *The High Cost of Business Disruption in Modifying and Maintaining ERP,* 2013.

Kahan, Dan, Peters, Ellen, Dawson, Erica and Slovic, Paul. *Motivated Numeracy and Enlightened Self-Government.* September 3, 2013.
   http://papers.ssrn.com/sol3/papers.cfm?abstract_id=2319992.

Kanaracus, Chris. *Air Force Scraps Massive ERP Project After Racking Up $1 Billion in Cost.* November 14, 2012.
   http://www.cio.com/article/721628/Air_Force_scraps_massive_ERP_project_after_racking_up_1_billion_in_costs.

Kimberling, Eric. *Are Two-Tier ERP Systems Finally Becoming Mainstream?* December 19, 2012.
   http://panorama-consulting.com/are-two-tier-erp-systems-finally-becoming-mainstream/.

Legacy System. Accessed October 28, 2013.
   http://en.wikipedia.org/wiki/Legacy_system.

List of Countries by Total Health Expenditure Per Capita. September 1, 2013.
   http://en.wikipedia.org/wiki/List_of_countries_by_total_health_expenditure_(PPP)_per_capita.

List of Largest Companies by Revenue. Last modified November 16, 2013.
   http://en.wikipedia.org/wiki/List_of_largest_companies_by_revenue.

Logical Fallacies. Accessed October 28, 2013.
    http://en.wikipedia.org/wiki/List_of_fallacies.

Mallory, James. *ERP Budget & Cost Considerations: Moving from QuickBooks to ERP.*
    http://blog.e2benterprise.com/erp-budget-cost-considerations-moving-from-quickbooks-to-erp-part-5-of-8-part-series/.

Mann, Charles. *Why Software Is Bad.* Technology Review. July 1, 2002.
    http://www.technologyreview.com/featuredstory/401594/why-software-is-so-bad/.

Mar, Anna. *12 Mind Bending ERP Statistics.* September 11, 2011.
    http://simplicable.com/new/12-mind-bending-ERP-statistics.

Markus, M. Lynne. *Enterprise Resource Planning: Multisite ERP Implementations. Association for Computing Machinery.* April 1, 2000.

Moon, Andy. *Are the Rewards of ERP Systems Worth the Risk.* March 27, 2008.
    http://www.techrepublic.com/blog/it-news-digest/are-the-rewards-of-erp-systems-worth-the-risk/.

Murry, Christopher. *Ranking 37th: Measuring the Performance of the U.S. Health Care System.* January 14, 2010.
    http://www.nejm.org/doi/full/10.1056/NEJMp0910064.

Nystrom, Christiana and Windler, Maria. *ERP System and Effects: A Comparison of Theory and Practice.* Gotenborg University, 2003.

Olsen, Art. *ERP: Repair or Replace.* April 1, 2013.
    http://www.pcbennettconsulting.com/erp-repair-or-replace/.

Opportunity Cost. Accessed June 22, 2013.
    https://en.wikipedia.org/wiki/Opportunity_cost.

Pabo-Nazao, Placid and Raymond, Louis *In House Development as an Alternative for ERP Adoption by SMES: A Critical Case Study,* 2009.

Perera, David. *Air Force Considering Alternatives to Key ERP.* October 30, 2011.
    http://www.fiercegovernmentit.com/story/air-force-considering-alternatives-key-erp/2011-10-30.

Philips, Steven Scott. *Control Your ERP Destiny: Reduce Project Costs, Mitigate Risks, and Design Better Business Solutions.* Street Smart ERP Publications, 2012.

Process Industry ERP Requirements. Wonderware, 2000.

Propaganda. October 28, 2013. http://en.wikipedia.org/wiki/Propaganda.

Prouty, Kevin and Castellina, Nick. *To ERP or Not to ERP*. April 2011.
http://www.plex.com/wordpress/wp-content/uploads/2012/05/Aberdeen-ERPvsNoERP.pdf.

Proving a Negative. Accessed March 15, 2013.
http://en.wikipedia.org/wiki/Proving_a_negative.

Radding, Alan. *ERP: More Than an Application*. Information Week, 1999.

Rettig, Cynthia. *The Trouble With Enterprise Software*. MIT Sloan, Fall 2007.
http://sloanreview.mit.edu/article/the-trouble-with-enterprise-software/.

Rich, Michael. *Standards for High-Quality Research and Analysis,* November 2011.
http://www.rand.org/standards.html.

Rohm, Ted. *To ERP or Not to ERP, that Is the C-Level Question*. February 22, 2013.
http://blog.technologyevaluation.com/blog/2013/02/22/to-erp-or-not-to-erp-that-is-the-c-level-question/.

Rokohl, Laura. *Visibility and Integration—The Key Ingredients for a Successful Supply Chain*. AspenTech. 2012.

Ross, J.W. *The ERP revolution: Surviving versus thriving*. MIT White Paper, November 1998.

Sabre (Computer System). Accessed July 16, 2013.
http://en.wikipedia.org/wiki/Sabre_(computer_system).

Savitz, Eric. *The End of ERP*. February 9, 2012.
http://www.forbes.com/sites/ciocentral/2012/02/09/the-end-of-erp/2/.

Singleton, Derek. *A Chronicle or ERP Software History Pt. II*. December 8, 2011.
http://ctovision.com/2011/12/a-chronicle-of-erp-software-history-pt-ii/.

Slater, Derek and Koch, Christopher. *The ABC's of ERP*.
http://paginas.fe.up.pt/~mgi00011/ERP/abcs_of_erp.htm.

Snapp, Shaun. *Enterprise Software Selection: How to Pinpoint the Perfect Software Solution Using Multiple Information Sources*. SCM Focus Press, 2013.

Snapp, Shaun. *Enterprise Software TCO: Calculating and Using Total Cost of Ownership for Decision Making,* SCM Focus Press, 2013.

Snapp, Shaun. *Gartner and the Magic Quadrant: A Guide for Buyers, Vendors, Investors,* SCM Focus Press, 2013.

Snapp, Shaun. *Process Industry Manufacturing Software: ERP, Planning, Recipe, MES & Process Control*. SCM Focus Press, 2013.

Snapp, Shaun. *Replacing Big ERP: Breaking the Big ERP Habit with Best-of-Breed Applications at a Fraction of the Cost.* SCM Focus Press, 2013.

Snapp, Shaun. *SuperPlant: Creating a Nimble Manufacturing Enterprise with Adaptive Planning Software.* SCM Focus Press. 2013.

Snapp, Shaun. *Supply Planning with MRP, DRP and APS Software.* SCM Focus Press, 2012.

Snapp, Shaun. *The Real Story Behind Two-tiered ERP.* SCM Focus Press, 2014.

Sommer, Brian. *ERP's Franken-soft and How Workday Avoids it.* November 13, 2012. http://www.zdnet.com/erps-franken-soft-and-how-workday-avoids-it-7000007200/.

Stanley, George. *4 ERP Tips for FIAR Compliance*, 2013.

Stein, Tom. *Making ERP Add Up.* Information Week, 1999.

Stross, Randall. *Billion-Dollar Flop: Air Force Stumbles on Software Plan.* New York Times. December 8, 2012. http://www.nytimes.com/2012/12/09/technology/air-force-stumbles-over-software-modernization-project.html?_r=0.

Study Finds Antidepressants to be Depressingly Ineffective. August 2, 2012. http://www.globalhealingcenter.com/natural-health/study-finds-antidepressants-to-be-depressingly-ineffective/.

Tautology. Accessed June 27, 2013. http://en.wikipedia.org/wiki/Tautology_(rhetoric).

The Depressing News About Antidepressants. Newsweek. January 28, 2010. http://mag.newsweek.com/2010/01/28/the-depressing-news-about-antidepressants.html.

The Promise of ERP Systems. Enterprise Systems for Higher Education. Vol. 4, 2002.

Two-tier Enterprise Resource Planning. Accessed August 29, 2013. http://en.wikipedia.org/wiki/Enterprise_resource_planning#Two_tier_enterprise_resource_planning.

Wagner, David. *Old & Bad ERP All Over Manufacturing.* April 17, 2013. http://www.enterpriseefficiency.com/author.asp?section_id=1151&doc_id=262241.

Wailgum, Thomas. *ERP Sticker Shock: Maintenance, Upgrades and Customizations.* September 23, 2010. http://www.cio.com/article/618117/ERP_Sticker_Shock_Maintenance_Upgrades_and_Customizations.

Wailgum, Thomas. *SaaS ERP Has Buzz, But Who Are the Real Players?* March 10, 2010. http://www.cio.com/article/572463/SaaS_ERP_Has_Buzz_But_Who_Are_the_Real_Players.

Wailgum, Thomas. *Want to Save $10 Million or More on ERP? Don't Buy Oracle or SAP.* February 26, 2009. http://blogs.cio.com/thomas_wailgum/want_to_save_10_million_or_more_on_erp_dont_buy_oracle_or_sap?source=nlt_cioenterprise.

Wainewright, Phil. *ERP, RIP? Cloud Financials and Revenue Management in 2013.* January 4, 2013. http://www.zdnet.com/erp-rip-cloud-financials-and-revenue-management-in-2013-7000009376/.

Weill, Peter. *The Relationship Between Investment in Information Technology and Firm Performance: A Study of the Valve Manufacturing Sector.* December 1992.

What is ERP? Netsuite. August 27, 2001. http://www.netsuite.com/portal/resource/articles/erp/what-is-erp.shtml.

Wolpe, Toby. *When SAP Sprawl is Cool: Could Cutting Back your ERP be More Pain than It's Worth?* May 9, 2013. http://www.zdnet.com/are-businesses-wasting-millions-on-sap-erp-they-dont-need-7000015133/.

Wood, Bill. *Overcome SAP-ERP System Integrator Sales Tactics.* May 9, 2011. http://www.r3now.com/overcoming-sap-erp-system-integrator-sales-tactics-1/.

Worthen, Ben. *Extreme ERP Makeover.* December 9, 2003. http://www.cio.com.au/article/181834/extreme_erp_makeover/?pp=5.

Year 2000 Problem. Accessed August 29, 2013. http://en.wikipedia.org/wiki/Year_2000_problem.